The Human Right to Peace

The Human Right to Peace

Douglas Roche

NOVALIS

Cover: Blair Turner
Cover image: Mitch Hrdlicka/Getty Images
Layout: Caroline Gagnon

Business Office:
Novalis
49 Front Street East, 2nd Floor
Toronto, Ontario, Canada
M5E 1B3

Phone: 1-877-702-7773 or (416) 363-3303
Fax: 1-877-702-7775 or (416) 363-9409
E-mail: cservice@novalis.ca
www.novalis.ca

National Library of Canada Cataloguing in Publication Data

Roche, Douglas, 1929–
    The human right to peace / Douglas Roche.

Includes index.
ISBN 2-89507-409-7

    1. Peace. 2. Human rights. I. Title.

JZ5538.R62 2003   327.1'72   C2003-904092-5

Printed in Canada.

We acknowledge the financial support of the Government of Canada through the Book Publishing Industry Development Program (BPIDP) for our publishing activities.

5   4   3   2   1   07   06   05   04   03

For Patricia McGoey

Contents

They shall beat their swords into plowshares,
and their spears into pruning hooks;
nation shall not lift up sword against nation,
neither shall they learn war any more.

—Isaiah 2:4

"We have entered the third millennium
through a gate of fire."

—Kofi Annan
United Nations Secretary-General
December 10, 2001
Nobel Peace Prize Lecture

Acknowledgments

Writing this book took only a few months, but thinking about the themes of the human right to peace has occupied my attention for a much longer period. For thirty years, I have been attending meetings and conferences at the United Nations in New York, Geneva, and elsewhere, including a period as Canada's Ambassador for Disarmament. The United Nations has been for me a school as well as a centre for world negotiations. I have benefited from the catalogue of information about the planet that the UN provides as well as the numerous officials who have befriended me with their confidences. No day is complete for me until I check the UN Web site, <www.un.org>, which contains valuable information on current events that is routinely bypassed by the general media.

In preparing this book, Todd Martin, my Research Assistant, helped assemble and organize my material, found important statistics, and proved an incisive critic of early drafts. He researched the list of informative Web sites at the end of the book.

Pam Miles-Séguin, my Administrative Assistant, once again enabled me to operate in two cities, Edmonton and Ottawa, at the same time. My work in the Senate had to go on during the writing of the book, and Pam made this possible. We have worked together for many years, and I have come to rely on her judgment as well as hard work in the presentation of my ideas in public forums.

As she has in past books, Bonnie Payne processed several drafts of this one in her efficient and cheerful manner. I thank all my staff. This book could not have been accomplished without them.

I am also indebted to David Adams, the former UNESCO official who for many years directed the organization's work on the culture of peace. He provided valuable research material to me, and read an early draft of Chapters 4, 5, and 6. John Burroughs, Executive Director of the Lawyers Committee for Nuclear Policy, gave me helpful criticism on nuclear weapons issues. Any errors in the book are, of course, my responsibility.

I also received help from the Library of Parliament and its Research Branch, especially Hugh Finsten and his staff. Arun Elhance, of the World Conference on Religion and Peace, provided helpful information on religious themes.

Ruth Bertelson, as she has with my previous books, gave me the confidence to proceed with this one.

Kevin Burns, my editor at Novalis, proved an unexpected joy. His perception of what I was trying to do, his support, and his easy manner of deepening my insights, sustained me greatly. I also appreciate the additional editing by Ellen Shenk.

Finally, my wife, Patricia McGoey, provided immense and constant support for me throughout the lonely hours of the writing process. I thank her with all my heart.

Edmonton, May 8, 2003

Introduction

Moving to Creativity

The world faces no greater challenge today than the challenge to end its relentless march to war. War causes starvation, deepens poverty, ruins environments, forces migrations of peoples, wrecks the rule of law, multiplies the gap between rich and poor, and causes prolonged misery for the most vulnerable people. Though these world problems are rooted in a host of factors, none can be resolved adequately unless we end the dominance of the culture of war.

In the twentieth century, at least 110 million people were killed in 250 wars. This is six times the number of war-related deaths as in the previous century. More than six million people have died in war since the end of the Cold War, when global security should have improved. The twenty-first century does not offer many prospects for improvement. In 2001 alone, 37 armed conflicts were fought in 30 countries. More than 600 million small arms are in circulation around the world, and they have been used to kill 500,000 people a year.

Some hold that war is a perpetual reality in this world, and that those who want to end war are mere idealists. I challenge that notion. War is not in the human genes. We are not predestined to violence. Rather, war comes out of our culture—the way we are socialized to interact with one another.

The central idea of this book is that the culture of war can and must be changed into a culture of peace. Work to accomplish this is already going on, but it is often drowned out by the drumbeats of war. Those who engage in peace work are the true realists of our time, for they understand that new technologies are accelerating the spread of weapons of mass destruction and, with them, the capacity to end life on earth. Today's idealists are those who think the status quo—the war culture—can be sustained without a world-wide calamity.

This book is built on my experiences and observations through four decades as a journalist, parliamentarian, diplomat, and educator. Throughout that time, I have been struck by the increased reliance on violence and war as the primary means of resolving political disputes, despite the existence of the machinery of peace. Though the United Nations (UN) and other regional security organizations provide a structure to find peaceful political solutions, the most powerful nations and the not so powerful still cling to the culture of war. Sub-state actors have taken up war with a vengeance.

The terrorist attacks of September 11, 2001, resulted in a surge of the war culture. The response to these attacks was war in Afghanistan and, by extension, war in Iraq in 2003. Both countries have become a tragic showcase of the tendency to use overwhelming violence in dealing with complex problems. For Iraq, the consequences of this recourse to war will reverberate loudly, and unpredictably, throughout the Middle East and beyond for years to come.

We are now facing a turning point. Terrorists anywhere can covertly destroy the prized assets of the powerful, and the powerful can invoke a new doctrine of pre-emptive attack to protect themselves. We need to face up to a hard reality: neither raw military strength, nuclear weapons, nor missile defences will defend us against persons who lash out at humanity itself because of their consuming hatred. Such hatred exploits the brutalities of the poverty, oppression, power, and greed of modern society. The powerful need to learn about the causes of that hatred. They need to understand that their best long-range defence lies in addressing the great injustices that are today increasing the divisions between rich and poor, the powerful and the vulnerable, and the triumphant and the despairing.

At the UN Millennium Summit in 2000, world leaders pledged to cut poverty in half by 2015. UN Secretary-General Kofi Annan requested $50 billion per year to achieve the Millennium Goals. Yet governments, pleading that they did not have the resources, pledged less than a quarter of this amount. Despite this stated inability to pay for development, governments have spent more than $10 trillion on armaments since 1990, the benchmark year for the end of the Cold War. Calculating how many schools, water and sanitation plants, health facilities, and environmental clean-up operations could have been built for even one-tenth of this $10 trillion staggers the imagination. An immense double standard prevails: in one breath, governments plead an inability to fund social and environmental needs, and in the next breath, they appropriate huge sums to prepare and execute warfare. The modern world countenances pumping trillions of dollars into armaments, while hundreds of millions of people face homelessness, starvation, grinding poverty, and a despoiled environment. These are breeding grounds for future conflicts, and glossing over the immensity of these violations to social justice does not serve truth well.

Of course, the past few decades have seen positive gains for humanity. The world economy has soared. Science has blossomed. Medical advances are stunning. Knowledge can be instantly transmitted by electronic means. However, the persons who enjoy these gains, for the most part, are already well off, and the gap between them and the dispossessed continues to grow. Despite all the advances in science and technology, injustice prevails. Although there is more than enough food to feed the six billion people of the world, fully one in six is actually underfed or starving, and hundreds die daily. UN Secretary-General Annan has issued a dire warning:

> The century just ended was disfigured, time and again, by ruthless conflict. Grinding poverty and striking inequality persist within and among countries even amidst unprecedented wealth. Diseases, old and new, threaten to undo painstaking progress. Nature's life-sustaining services, on which our species depends for its survival, are being seriously disrupted and degraded by our own everyday activities.

World population will increase by two billion over the next 25 years, and 95 per cent of that growth will occur in societies already weighed down with poverty, wars, and environmental degradation. The rich–poor gap, the proliferation of weapons large and small, the ethnic hatreds, the environmental destruction, the forced migration of peoples—none of these are sustainable. We must understand that these negative trends lead to more conflict, calamitous suffering, widespread social disorder, and ruination of whole sections of the planet.

This assessment of the world and its future is not just a matter of statistics and abstractions. My view of the world has been shaped by my experiences. I have walked through disease-ridden slums and shantytowns of Africa, Asia, and Latin America. I have held a dying Indian baby in my arms. I have seen gaunt bodies, despoiled lands, and the wreckage of Hiroshima. But I have also been in villages in Bangladesh where child deaths were wiped out by a simple but effective UN Children's Fund (UNICEF) oral rehydration program. I have been part of international negotiations where progress toward disarmament was made inch by inch. I have been lifted up by the chorus of world leaders calling for a better world, only to be deflated by the absurd skewing of governmental priorities that emphasize war preparations while starving peace processes.

I am outraged at the political duplicity of the powerful, who speak of equality and peace but rely on military means to force their will. I am critical of the hypocrisies that justify a political and economic system that spends countless sums on endless wars but cannot feed and educate every child in the world. It is not right to spend $60 billion on a needless and unworkable missile defence system when that same amount could provide adequate water and sanitation to the two billion people who lack both.

Merely railing against injustice does not accomplish much. But what accomplishes even less is closing our eyes to the massive discrepancies and assuming that the culture of war is sustainable. Action is urgently needed. The goal must be to build a world system that will make war extinct.

A distinguishing feature of our time is that morality and pragmatism have intersected. What we have long known we *should* do for our brothers and sisters on the planet, we now know we *must* do to ensure our very survival. Humanity has no other option. It is not news that moral teaching emphasizes the core values of respect for life, liberty, justice, and equity; a mutual respect; and personal integrity. What is news is that technology has brought us to the point where we all stand on one planet, breathe the same air, are affected by one another's problems, and possess the power to annihilate each other. The physical integrity of all human life today demands political policies that enhance, not diminish, life. The common good requires policies that promote sustainable and socially equitable development and peace in all regions of the globe.

I want a world that is human-centred and genuinely democratic—a world that builds and protects peace, equality, justice, and development. I want a world where human security, as envisioned in the principles of the UN Charter, replaces armaments, violent conflict, and wars. I want a world where everyone lives in a clean environment with a fair distribution of the earth's resources and where human rights are protected by a body of international law.

I am not alone in these desires, for this is the precise agenda advanced by the People's Millennium Forum held at the UN in 2000. The rise of civil society groups that define their claim to a more just world is another sign of the times. The work of committed non-governmental organizations (NGOs) has undoubtedly strengthened the UN's ability to develop many kinds of programs. These include providing universal education, improving health and nutrition for children, protecting the environment, providing human rights, protecting reproductive health, eradicating poverty, advancing and empowering women, improving human settlements, and providing wide-ranging arms control. Examples of success are the role of civil society in the Campaign to Ban Landmines and in developing the International Criminal Court.

A new culture of peace agenda is already underway. It is challenging the culture of war. True, the forces of the culture of war have, for the moment, the upper hand. They have the levers of power. But the number of creative, active people working for a better world continues to increase. The millions of people around the world who marched before and during the Iraq war of 2003 are a sign of this activism. The Dalai Lama recently noted:

> We are witnessing a tremendous popular movement for the advancement of human rights and democratic freedom in the world. This movement must become an even more powerful moral force, so that even the most obstructive governments and armies are incapable of suppressing it.

As the world continues to develop a culture of peace, the human right to peace will come into view more clearly. The UN has already defined the concept of peace as a human right, but its meaning has been muted by the continuation of the war culture. The very agonies of war and the dark night of suffering that has lasted for centuries are awakening civilization to a new understanding: the peoples of the Earth have a sacred right to peace. The object of this book is to explore and animate the concept of peace as a human right so that it can finally take its place among the other human rights recognized by the international system.

Before we examine the development of the culture of peace and the subsequent right to peace, we must deepen our understanding of how deeply the culture of war permeates our lives. We must stand back for a moment and look at ourselves and at what we are doing to the planet. The photograph of earth sent back by the astronauts in space, one of the icons of the twentieth century, helps us to understand human unity, but the photograph of the mushroom cloud over Hiroshima offsets it. One shows the creativity of humanity; the other its destructiveness. To move to creativity, we must shine a light on world conditions. Only then can we appreciate how we must change our attitudes toward war and peace.

In a world where our destinies are increasingly held in common, a culture of peace can bring genuine hope to the lives of the many millions who need and want to be lifted up from the horrors of daily life. We must build a just world if humanity is to survive. And that survival calls us to reject out of hand the cynicism and despair that crush hope and vision.

PART I

The Culture of War

1

Violence as a Way of Life

World War I, from 1914 to 1918, was the first mass global war of the industrialized age. Fought in stinking trenches that stretched from the English Channel to the Swiss frontier, it claimed ten million lives. Although popular opinion has it that the war was caused by the assassination of Archduke Franz Ferdinand of Austria-Hungary, its origins actually lie in the aggressive stance taken by Kaiser Wilhelm II of Germany against the Entente Powers led by Great Britain. The Kaiser's bellicosity led to a bloodbath never before experienced, with losses in life per day exceeding 5,500. For the first time, whole societies were organized for war, the great majority of people supporting it because they believed that victory for their own country was worth the cost. It was called "the war to end all wars." How wrong that was.

Adolf Hitler rose to power in Germany in the early 1930s and began to rearm a country that had not even recovered from World War I. When Hitler invaded Poland in 1939, Britain responded with a declaration of war. Before this war ended in 1945, it had claimed the lives of 15 million combatants and 35 million civilians. No fewer than 56 countries were involved in what became the most destructive conflict in history. The Soviet Union alone suffered 20 million casualties. More than six million Jews and five million others were murdered in the Nazi Germany concentration camps. Cities and industries across Europe and Japan were reduced to rubble. Never before had a war so fundamentally affected the lives of civilians, who were bombed mercilessly. The atomic bombing of Hiroshima, which alone took 140,000 lives, ushered the world into the frightening nuclear weapons era.

Hardly five years after the end of World War II, troops from Communist North Korea invaded South Korea. The UN force, composed largely of South Korean and American troops, pushed North Korea back. China entered the conflict. Before an armistice was signed in 1953, the dead soldiers numbered 1,500,000.

In Vietnam, what began as a small US involvement to help South Vietnam resist an internal insurgency mounted by the Viet Cong (supported by Communist North Vietnam) soon escalated to the deployment of 540,000 US troops by 1968. The US engaged in massive saturation bombing campaigns and deliberately destroyed the environment in attempts to root out enemy forces. One million Vietnamese perished and 58,000 US troops were killed. In the end, the South fell to the North. The war had a profound effect on the American psyche, as many questioned the fundamental rationale for the war and were hesitant to support the deployment of US forces to future crises.

Four years of mass genocide in Cambodia in the 1970s resulted in two million deaths. The Iran–Iraq war of the 1980s left one million dead. The 1992–95 war in Bosnia killed 200,000 and accounted for two million refugees, many of whom were terrorized and forced from their home regions in co-ordinated "ethnic cleansing" campaigns. Somalia, Rwanda, Sierra Leone, the Congo, Kosovo, Afghanistan, Iraq—in the past ten years all of these places have become synonymous with war. In 2001, 37 armed conflicts took place in 30 countries; 75 per cent had begun more than a decade ago, which means that entire generations of children are growing up in environments fraught with extreme violence and poverty. In some conflicts, civilians have been mutilated as part of a deliberate strategy to demoralize communities and destroy their social structures. Prime examples are the civil wars in Mozambique and Sierra Leone, where many people had ears, lips, or limbs severed by rebels. Genocides, rapes, mutilations, bombings, and famines have become the standard for countless persons caught in the senseless patterns of conflict.

While the world spotlight was on the Iraq war of 2003, "silent wars," ignored by the major media, were fought in many places: the Ivory Coast, Liberia, Nigeria, Kashmir, the Philippines. The Great Lakes region of Africa, particularly the Congo, is witnessing constant massacres and bloodshed. Continued violence between Palestinian and Israeli forces scars the Holy Land. The wars in all these regions are devastating for the people in the area, yet international attention is sporadic.

Wars are no longer about soldiers killing soldiers. Civilians constitute the new front line in today's conflicts. It is inexpressibly sad that in the past decade two million children have been killed in conflict, and millions more have been disabled, made orphans, and left with severe psychological trauma. Some 800 children are killed or maimed by land mines every month. Throughout 50 countries, 20 million children have been left homeless by war. Girls are especially vulnerable. Girls in Rwanda suddenly became the heads of some 60,000 households following the genocide in that country. Girls from the Balkans have been trafficked into prostitution rings in Western Europe. School girls have been abducted in Northern Uganda. Militias exist whose preferred suicide commandos are girls.

The spectacle of child soldiers is another example of the callousness of our time. Some 300,000 youths under age 18 have fought in recent years in conflicts ranging from Sri Lanka to Colombia, from Chechnya to Sudan. The widely used AK-47 assault rifle, for example, can be easily carried and used to deadly effect by children as young as ten. *The New York Times* recently reported that in the Ivory Coast—a country rich with cocoa, timber, and diamonds—"guns are as plentiful as mangoes in March, and longstanding tribal enmities are easily deployed. As are hungry, bored teenagers with a gun in hand and a chance to star in their own Schwarzenegger fantasies."

We often associate big and powerful weapons with modern warfare. While huge weapons abound, most of the killing today is done with small arms: machine guns, rifles, and pistols. Civil wars in Uganda, Ethiopia, Somalia, and Sudan have ushered in a boom in the illegal market in small arms. These weapons are now being used in conflicts over natural resources and cattle rustling, and have contributed to soaring violent crime rates in cities such as Nairobi, Mogadishu, and Kigali. Due to porous and expansive borders, weak governments, and ineffective national security systems, the movement of small arms is difficult to control or account for as they progress within the region from one conflict to another. Their use goes far beyond armies and police forces to criminal organizations, private security forces, vigilante squads, and individual citizens. The manufacture of these weapons has risen sharply and is widespread. A survey by the Graduate Institute of International Studies in Geneva estimates that 1,000 companies in 98 countries produced the 639 million small arms that are in circulation today. The trade in illicit arms swells this number. The biggest arms traders are the US, Russia, China, the UK, France, and Germany—some of the strongest countries in the world that ought not to be dependent on this nefarious business.

War Is Profitable—For Some

To the human toll of warfare must be added the economic cost and the lost opportunities for economic and social development. The total cost of warfare in the twentieth century is probably impossible to calculate; the figure, if it existed, would be incomprehensible. There is a hint of this cost in the figure of \$5.5 trillion, which *Atomic Audit* established as the amount spent by the US solely for developing nuclear weapons between 1940 and 1997. Worldwide development of weapons of mass destruction has cost many times that amount. UN documents through the years have criticized high military budgets as a waste and misuse of resources, but the criticism is usually couched in general terms. The major states, the most profligate, are never named because they control the agenda of inter-national meetings where UN documents are presented. A world spotlight should be put on the G8 (the US, the UK, France, Russia, Germany, Japan, Italy, and Canada), the richest and most powerful countries in the world. Together the G8 holds 98 per cent of all nuclear weapons, is responsible for 75 per cent of annual world military expenditures, and accounts for 87 per cent of the weapons trade.

The US dwarfs the rest of the world in military spending. The 2003 US defence budget of \$400 billion is six times larger than that of Russia, the second largest spender, and more than the combined spending of the next 25 nations. It is 26 times larger than the combined spending of the seven countries the US refers to as "rogue states" (Cuba, Iran, Iraq, Libya, North Korea, Sudan, and Syria); these states are identified by the Pentagon as the most likely US adversaries.

The bond between the US military establishment and defence corporations brought into existence the "military-industrial complex," which US President Dwight Eisenhower first warned about in 1961. This destruction industry has increased enormously in power in the succeeding four decades and is now the dominant player in the US economy. Military orders for lethal weapons, surveillance equipment, tanks, submarines, ships, and airplanes drive America's manufacturing sector. More than one-third of all engineers and scientists in the US are engaged in military-related jobs. Several sectors of the country and a number of industrial sectors, particularly shipbuilding and aerospace, are very dependent on military spending and foreign arms sales.

The Afghanistan and Iraq wars have been a boon to the arms industry. Despite a sluggish economy elsewhere in the last quarter of 2002, the Lockheed Martin Corporation, the No. 2 military contractor, reported a 6 per cent rise in sales, highlighted by its F/A-22 fighter jets, each with a $200 million price tag. The Raytheon Company, maker of the Stinger and Tomahawk missiles, reported that its operating profits had more than doubled. The political power of the military-industrial complex dwarfs ordinary lobbyists in Washington. Not only are the political campaigns of many politicians funded by such companies, once in office these legislators find it virtually impossible to say no to the demands of the military-industrial complex to approve new weapons systems. The current development of a missile defence system and plans to put weapons in space will represent, for this industry, a bottomless pit of wealth.

What drives military spending? The traditional answer lies in the need for national security. But that is only a small part of the answer. The insatiable demands of the military-industrial complex are another, and major, reason. War is definitely profitable for the sprawling defence industries around the world. So is the fear-mongering in which politicians indulge when they capitalize on the uncertainties in the modern world. The core of the answer, however, lies in the dominance of a culture of war. When I use this term, a synonym for militarism, I mean the exaltation of military values in the resolution of conflict, which leads to aggressive military preparedness and a dominant political status for the military.

Cultural Roots of Violence

Where, then, does war come from? Why do we have it? The Carnegie Commission on Preventing Deadly Conflict examined this question and found that deadly conflict is not inevitable. Violence on the scale of the wars of the twentieth century does not emerge inexorably from human interaction. Rather, war and mass violence usually result from deliberate political decisions. Violent conflict has often resulted from the traditional preoccupation of governments to defend, maintain, or extend their interests and power. The Commission found:

> Many factors and conditions make societies prone to warfare: weak, corrupt, or collapsed states; illegitimate or repressive regimes; acute discrimination against ethnic or other social groups; poorly managed religious, cultural, or ethnic differences; politically active religious communities that promote hostile and divisive messages; political and economic legacies of colonialism or the Cold War; sudden economic and political shifts; widespread illiteracy, disease, and disability; lack of resources such as water and arable land; large stores of weapons and ammunition; and threatening regional relationships. When long-standing grievances are exploited by political demagogues, the scene is set for violence.

The problem of violence in wars must be seen in a much wider context than the mere act of aggression. The roots of violent conflict are generally deep and often the result of long-standing tensions between groups. The Carnegie Commission identified a number of factors that put states at risk of violent conflict. They include:

1) A lack of democratic processes and unequal access to power; social inequality marked by grossly unequal distribution of, and access to, resources;

2) Control by a single national group of valuable natural resources, such as gems, oil, timber, and drugs;

3) Rapid demographic change that outstrips the capacity of the state to provide essential services and job opportunities;

4) The availability of weapons.

War also requires an enemy. It requires armaments and soldiers. It requires control of information. Not least, it requires a belief that power can be obtained or maintained by violence. This is so deeply imbedded in our thinking that we refuse to invest either sufficient money or confidence in non-violent ways to guarantee peace. No country or community is untouched by this tendency toward violence. Images and accounts of violence pervade the media: violence is on our streets and in our homes, schools, workplaces, and institutions. Violence is a universal scourge that tears at the fabric of communities and threatens the life, health, and happiness of all. A study by the World Health Organization found that violence kills 1.6 million people each year through wars, murders, and suicide.

Unfortunately, we have become conditioned to violence. The daily headlines no longer shock us. We take them for granted and often do not even think about them. Most people probably think of themselves as non-violent persons, but when people's human rights are violated and we do not speak up we are condoning violence. We accept the use of violence when we are willing to live under policies that threaten the use of nuclear weapons against people we do not even know and with whom we have no quarrel. We excuse violence against the poor around the world who are discriminated against by economic policies designed by the rich. We have become so accustomed to violence that our senses have been numbed. True, we were shocked at the deaths of innocent civilians in the events of September 11, 2001, but that was also because of the spectacular nature of these attacks against the world's superpower. People in many parts of the world are the victims of war and other injustices without the same outcry or media coverage. Some 30,000 children die every day from malnutrition and easily controllable diseases—a form of violence in itself.

We even willingly pay for violence in the form of entertainment, at the movies and video rental stores. Turn on a television and we are constantly reminded of violence by the media, with daily reports of violent crimes. Violence is also a staple of fiction. By the time the average child turns 18, he or she will have watched 8,000 murders and more than 100,000 acts of violence on TV screens alone. Violence is now depicted in a variety of formats—including video and virtual reality games, Internet sites, and satellite TV channels. Media, including films, are, in fact, polluted with violence and distortions of reality. Although the connection between media violence and aggressive behaviour is very much in dispute, the fact remains that media portrayals of violence have grown exponentially over the past few decades. And, what is equally disturbing, this development has subsumed portrayals of peaceful social behaviour. The Pentagon values its connections to Hollywood, whose glamorization of war provides better box office returns than anti-war movies. Drug and alcohol abuse, suicide, cult worship, serial killing, racism, sexism, random violence, and general bigotry are widely depicted in many TV shows, films, and popular music. Messages on values, good examples, and character formation have all become secondary to the inevitability of violence. The seductive power of violence infuses children's minds, and the media portrayal of violence becomes the reference point for future life experiences. Is it any wonder that as adults they accept violence as a part of life?

So deep-seated are the roots of violence that many people think that violence is an ingrained part of human nature. According to this logic, we will always have war and we can do no better than to mitigate the worst aspects of violence. This is a superficial analysis. We are not genetically programmed for war. There is no inherent biological component of our nature that produces violence. This is the conclusion of the Seville Statement on Violence drafted in 1986 by 20 leading biological and social scientists under the auspices of the International Society for Research on Aggression. (This statement deserves more attention than it has received in public debate. It can be found at www.unesco.org/cpp/uk/declarations/seville.pdf. Additional sources of information are listed in the notes to this chapter.)

After examining arguments based on evolution, genetics, animal behaviour, brain research, and social psychology, these scientists drew the conclusion that biology does not predestine us to war and violence. War, the scientists said, is a product of culture. There are cultures that have engaged in war for centuries, and there are cultures that have not waged war for centuries. The statement says it is scientifically incorrect to say that war or any other violent behaviour is genetically programmed into our human nature. It is also incorrect to say that humans have a "violent brain" or that war is caused by instinct or any single motivation.

> We conclude that biology does not condemn humanity to war, and that humanity can be freed from the bondage of biological pessimism ... . Just as 'wars begin in the minds of men,' peace also begins in our minds. The same species who invented war is capable of inventing peace. The responsibility lies with each of us.

Lifting ourselves out of the culture of war and toward a culture of peace has become even harder since September 11. Instant recourse to the war machine to pursue terrorists suddenly seemed to be justified. At least, that is how governments attempted to persuade their publics in the run-up to the bombing of Afghanistan. Knee-jerk violence in retaliation against violence came naturally. The culture of war needs an identifiable enemy, armaments and soldiers, control of information, and a belief that the use of violence will solve the conflict. The terrorists provided a new rationale for the war machine. The public, as if it were programmed, quickly accepted government rationale that more military spending was needed to produce ever more sophisticated and destructive weapons systems. And so the bombardment of Afghanistan started in the name of a "just war." *The Times* of London described the effects of one such attack on the Afghan village of Torai, as seen by a villager who was less than 2 kilometres (a mile) away at the time and described "a massive fireball rising from the ground."

> The roll call of the dead read like an invitation list to a family wedding: his mother-in-law, two sisters-in-law, three brothers-in-law, and four of his sister's five young children, two girls and two boys, all under the age of eight.

The Bombing of Afghanistan

The patterns of warfare in Afghanistan—warfare throughout its history and in the new war against terrorism—illustrate the chaos and suffering that always accompany war.

Afghanistan, a country of 28 million people roughly the size of Texas or Saskatchewan, is strategically located between the Middle East, Central Asia, and the Indian subcontinent along the ancient "Silk Route." Although most of the energy used in Afghani homes comes from firewood and other traditional fuels, the country has the largest untapped oil reserves in the world along its northern frontier, but poor infrastructure prevents access. The oil market remains a major factor in other countries' interest in Afghanistan.

Afghanistan has been invaded, conquered, burned out, and looted for most of its 5,000-year history. The Russians, Alexander the Great, Genghis Khan, the British, the Taliban, and now the Americans have attempted to tame its land and peoples at great cost. Five major tribes have warred with one another constantly. Most governments have risen to power through war, coups, and self-serving councils. The unifying factor is Islam. About 85 per cent of the people are Sunni Muslims, the rest Shiite. While many villages have no school at all, the estimates list one mosque for every 50 to 100 households. Only a third of the boys and 8 per cent of the girls receive any primary education. One out of every four Afghan children under five die of preventable disease. There is only one physician for every 50,000 people. Typhoid and cholera epidemics have been widespread.

Dire economic and health conditions have been exacerbated by political and military upheavals during the wars of the past two decades. In 1973, the government monarchy was overthrown in a military coup headed by the Communist party. A counter-coup in 1978 spurred the mujahedeen movement (funded by the US, Pakistan, and Saudi Arabia) against the Communists. The Soviet Union invaded in 1979, beginning a conflict that would ultimately claim 40,000 Soviet lives and an estimated one million Afghan lives during the ten-year occupation. Three million refugees fled to Pakistan and 1.5 million to Iran. During the war, the Soviets and the Americans spent $3 billion each supporting their respective proxies. The Soviets withdrew in 1989, the Americans left with the end of the Cold War, the mujahedeen splintered into seven factions, and the Taliban—a largely Pashtun movement—came to power. The Taliban were mostly sons and orphans of mujahedeen who had been raised in refugee camps in Pakistan and were opposed to what they saw as the corruption of the mujahedeen. By 1996, the Taliban had taken control of most of the country through violence and warfare.

The Taliban created one of the most repressive countries in the world, engaging in unparalleled human rights violations against its citizenry. Forced deportation of civilians, summary executions, abuse and arbitrary detention of civilians, and indiscriminate bombing were common. Children under fourteen were conscripted to fight. Taliban forces targeted particular religions and ethnic minorities in mass killings, and destroyed many of Afghanistan's cultural objects and historic architecture. They even blew up the two Bamiyan Buddhas, gigantic statues dating back to the fourth and sixth centuries, that UNESCO had declared a world heritage site. The media were severely restricted and Radio Afghanistan was renamed Radio Voice of Shari'ah (Islamic Law) to reflect the Islamic fundamentalist views held by the Taliban. Television was banned as a source of moral corruption and music regarded as suspect. Women were forced to cover themselves from head to toe in burkas (long, tent-like veils), forbidden to attend schools or work outside the home, and publicly beaten or stoned if they were improperly dressed or escorted by men not related to them.

The Taliban peddled arms to finance the regime, and provided a haven to Osama bin Laden, leader of the Al-Qaeda terrorist network, who used Afghanistan as a terrorist training ground. The US then labelled Afghanistan a rogue state for harbouring Osama bin Laden, who had been accused of bombing American embassies in Kenya and Tanzania. In response, the US launched cruise missiles in August 1998 at alleged terrorist training camps in eastern Afghanistan. The UN Security Council demanded that the Taliban stop providing sanctuary and training for international terrorists and their organizations, and co-operate in bringing indicted terrorists to justice. When the Taliban failed to respond, the UN imposed sanctions. The next year, 1999, the Security Council demanded that the Taliban hand over Osama bin Laden to appropriate authorities. The regime's refusal to do so allowed bin Laden to set in motion the deadliest terrorist attack ever on American soil on September 11.

The terrorist attacks on the World Trade Center and the Pentagon were a crime against humanity. The death count from these attacks and those who died in the hijacked planes in Pennsylvania, Washington D.C., and New York exceeded 3,000. Retaliation was demanded in the heat of the moment.

The Security Council quickly adopted a resolution authorizing "all necessary steps" to combat terrorism. The North Atlantic Treaty Organization (NATO) invoked Article 5 of its Charter, which commits all NATO members to respond to an attack on any one member. Thus the stage was quickly set to claim legal authority for a bombing campaign to root out Osama bin Laden and the Al-Qaeda network of terrorists in Afghanistan, suspected of masterminding the attacks. The fact that most of the terrorists who had hijacked the planes on September 11 were Saudi Arabians, had been living legally in the US, and had no connection with Afghanistan, was overlooked.

On October 7, 2001, the US, supported by a coalition of 27 states, began the aerial bombing of Afghanistan. The public was assured that the US-UK military planners would go to great lengths to avoid civilian casualties. Newer, precision-guided weapons would ensure that only "the bad guys" were killed. But the facts proved this assertion wrong. On October 21 alone, between 60 to 80 innocent Afghan civilians were killed by US bombs dropped in five provinces during six bombing incidents. The dead included families having breakfast in the Parod Gajaded neighbourhood of Kabul and 25 persons who were killed in the bombing of a one-time military hospital and mosque in Kerat. US authorities downplayed the number of civilian deaths, and the mainline media reported that much of the bombing was taking place in remote areas. The US bombed the Kabul office of Al Jazeera, the independent Arab television network. The Pentagon's denials of carnage, coupled with the general popularity of the war, accounted for much of the ignorance about what was really going on. Patriotism ruled the day. When images of levelled villages began appearing on American TV screens, CNN chairman Walter Isaacson sent a memo to his staff ordering them to balance reports of civilian destruction in Afghanistan with reminders that the Taliban had harboured terrorists. The memo said: "It seems perverse to focus too much on the casualties or hardship in Afghanistan."

The number of civilians killed by the bombing remains in dispute. Marc W. Herold, an author and professor at the University of New Hampshire, relying on media and NGO reports, says between 3,100 and 3,600 deaths occurred. Other estimates put the toll at between 500 and 1,000. What is indisputable is that the bombing dislocated the lives of many thousands of persons and destroyed an infrastructure that still needs rebuilding. The UN reported that up to 70 per cent of the population of three major Afghan cities was forced from their homes by the bombing. The bombing swelled the numbers of refugees in the border areas of Pakistan and Iran. The deaths and maiming of civilians were the result of US planning that chose to carry out a bombing campaign using extremely powerful weaponry. Dubious military targets were frequently chosen. Though civilians were not deliberately targeted, it is impossible in modern warfare to kill only enemy combatants. In fact, since the 1990s, 90 per cent of casualties in warfare have been civilian and only ten per cent military.

With the quick defeat of the Taliban and the signing of the Bonn Agreement, an interim government headed by Hamid Karzai was eventually formed and elections for a permanent government were scheduled for 2004. But Afghanistan is still in the hands of local warlords, fuelling ethnic conflict, and religious and political divisions. Factional armies and militia groups have re-emerged, underscoring the government's lack of authority over the country outside of Kabul. Even in Kabul, armed Afghans in olive fatigues, Kalashnikovs slung over their shoulders, harass and shake down people at will. Again, the age-old tendency toward violent confrontation has undermined the peace process, hampered economic progress, limited development assistance, and impaired the exercise of basic human rights.

The World Bank estimated that $10.2 billion over a period of five years would be needed to rebuild the country. Afghan authorities said at least $23 billion over five years was necessary. But donor countries pledged only $1.8 billion for 2002 and $4.5 billion over five years. The initial money was absorbed by the humanitarian needs of two million refugees, and only a tiny fraction has gone to long-term reconstruction. As a result, the government is having extreme difficulty paying salaries, running hospitals and schools, and, more generally, convincing its citizens of its own legitimacy. Distribution of aid outside Kabul is hampered by the perilous state of security.

The scale of human suffering in Afghanistan has given the lie to Western claims of beneficence. The truth is that the US and its allies easily found the tens of billions of dollars to wage war in Afghanistan, but cannot, or refuse to, find the money to reconstruct the wartorn society, including comprehensive disarmament programs. In Kabul, half a million people, including returning refugees, had no place to live during the winter of 2003. The country is still laden with land mines, the drug trade is on the rise, crime is rampant, and the rights of women and minorities are commonly violated. The struggle to pacify Afghanistan and put it on the long-term path to peace and development will take years of commitment and billions more dollars.

Afghanistan's culture of violence also has to take into account the countries around it, since Afghanistan forms the core of a wider regional conflict consuming its neighbours. This includes the continuing challenges in Tajikistan, the conflict spurred by the growing Islamic movement in Uzbekistan, political decay in Pakistan, challenges to political order in Iran, and the ongoing insurgency in Kashmir. Does the West care enough to stay for the long haul? Shortly after the Afghan war, the world's attention shifted to a war to overthrow Iraqi dictator Saddam Hussein. Again, billions of dollars were found overnight to pursue war. The US alone committed an initial $75 billion to war in Iraq. Afghanistan's needs have slipped from view. Meanwhile, a second generation of Afghans is now growing up displaced and abandoned, with little education, an impoverished environment flooded by light weapons, and criminality everywhere. What will be the result of such hopelessness and hatred? One can only imagine the anarchy in Afghanistan in the years ahead.

Violence Repeated in Iraq

Iraq's unique standing in the world goes back thousands of years. This "cradle of civilization" is the fabled land of the Hanging Gardens of Babylon, the legends of Scheherazade and the Arabian Nights, the playground of Lawrence of Arabia, and the site of the Bible's Garden of Eden. Endowed with the waters of the Tigris and Euphrates rivers and sitting atop the world's second-largest oil reserves, Iraq has been trampled by an endless march of foreigners hungry for the country's riches. Settled by the Sumerians in 5500 B.C., the area that makes up present-day Iraq has been the reluctant host to uninvited guests including the Assyrians, Persians, Greeks, Alexander the Great's Macedonians, Parthians, Romans, and Arab Muslims who created a vast Islamic empire stretching from Spain to China. Overrun by the Mongols and later swallowed up by the Ottoman Empire, modern Iraq began to take shape in the 1800s under British influence.

Britain's primary interest with the Persian Gulf region had been to protect its trade routes with India, but when oil was discovered in southern Persia (modern-day Iran) in 1908, British designs for the region quickly changed. Britain suffered close to 100,000 casualties when it took the Persian Gulf from the Ottoman Empire in 1917. With the creation of the Anglo-Persian Oil Company, Britain was assured an endless source of fuel to feed its sprawling empire. In 1920, the League of Nations gave Britain a mandate over the region, which was renamed "Iraq" (Arabic for "the well-rooted country") the following year. It was anything but.

Britain brushed aside all local sensibilities and drew borders based largely on the front lines of its troops at the end of World War I; these borders cut across religious, ethnic, and ideological lines. Cutting Kuwait off the southern part of the new country, the British created a practically landlocked country. The Shiite majority to the south of Baghdad, currently estimated at 60 per cent of the country's 23 million people, was subordinated to the Sunni minority, itself divided between Arabs and Kurds. London installed a new government led by an Arab, King Faisal I, but retained control of the country's army, foreign policy, finances, and oil reserves. Encountering stiff resistance over the next decade, Britain ceded power and Iraq gained independence in 1932. After King Faisal's death in 1933, tribal fighting broke out and anti-British groups gained influence.

With opposition to the monarchy hitting a breaking point, army officers overthrew the government in 1958 and declared Iraq a republic. General Abdul Karim Kassem proclaimed himself premier of the new republic and proceeded to reverse Iraq's pro-Western policies, moving the country closer to the communist nations. But ethnic unrest continued and, in 1963, members of the nationalist Baath Party assassinated Kassem and another army officer, Abdul Salam Arif, and seized control. Saddam Hussein emerged from the bowels of the Baath Party as an operative with a foggy past as an enforcer. By the time Hussein declared himself president in 1979 after a bloodless coup, he had transformed the party into the vehicle of his ruthless drive to power.

By the late 1970s, Iraq was the second-largest oil producer, boasted a modern infrastructure, and had the highest standard of living in the Middle East. It had an affluent middle class and one of the most sophisticated social service systems in the region. Literacy was rising to new levels and Iraq's desire for learning and culture was deepening. But this would not last.

Once in power, Hussein quickly zeroed in on Iran. The 1979 Iranian Revolution was of tremendous concern to Iraq. Iranian fundamentalists were supporting separatist Kurds in northern Iraq and attempting to inflame rebellion among Iraq's Shiite population in the south. Iraq invaded Iran in 1980, starting a conflict that would drag on for eight years, costing some 700,000 Iraqi and Iranian lives, and that damaged Iraqi oil facilities, ruined the country's economy and social infrastructure, and would alter the course of Iraqi history. Only Western and Soviet arms merchants reaped any benefit from the carnage. During the war, Hussein unleashed chemical weapons against enemy soldiers while the major powers looked on with barely a murmur. During the final stage of the war in 1987, Hussein launched the first of the chemical attacks on the Iraqi Kurds and, in 1988, the Kurdish village of Halabja was destroyed by chemical weapons, killing thousands. Altogether, Hussein's vicious campaign of revenge against Iraqi Kurds killed more than 100,000 and forced another 1.5 million from their homes.

Between 1981 and 1988, Hussein was able to purchase an estimated $46.7 billion worth of arms and military equipment from foreign suppliers, the largest accumulation ever of modern weaponry by a developing country, including chemical weapons and materials to make atomic bombs. Eighty per cent of these arms were imported from the five permanent members of the UN Security Council. At the time, Western diplomats called Hussein a force of moderation in the Middle East, despite his invasion of Iran and his treatment of minority groups in his own country. It was a US diplomat, April Gilespie, who, when asked by Saddam what the US would do if he invaded Kuwait, indicated that America had no interest in Iraq's border disputes. Citing disagreements over territory, oil production, and money owed, Iraq invaded Kuwait—its ally in the war against Iran—on August 2, 1990, and rapidly took over the small country. The UN Security Council issued twelve resolutions condemning the occupation, imposed an overarching trade embargo on Iraq, demanded that it withdraw unconditionally by January 15, 1991, and, when it refused, finally authorized the use of force. Led by the United States, Operation Desert Storm became the largest showcase of military power ever in the region. The 43-day war began on January 17, 1991, and was fought largely from the air with US warplanes flying some 100,000 bombing raids over Iraq. A massive 100-hour ground assault ensured a coalition victory, but not before Hussein's army started fires in 722 Kuwaiti oil wells and released the equivalent of 8 billion barrels of oil into the Persian Gulf. As Iraqi soldiers retreated back into Iraq, US aircraft repeatedly strafed the line of people and vehicles travelling along the highway from Kuwait into Iraq in what US forces openly boasted was a "turkey shoot." The US also used shells made of depleted uranium, believed responsible for a significant increase in cancer and birth defects in southern Iraq. All told, over 100,000 Iraqis died during the war, which also resulted in 367 American fatalities.

Toward the end of the war, and after deciding not to take Baghdad, then-President George H. Bush urged the Iraqi people to take matters into their own hands and force Hussein from power. Rebels quickly took control of Basra and other cities in the south where Shiite Muslims are the vast majority, and other southern provinces began to fall. Fearing southern Iraq would break away, the Bush Administration balked at helping the rebellion it had stirred up. This hesitation gave Hussein the time he needed to organize and crush the southern rebellion ruthlessly and viciously, killing some 30,000 Shiites, mostly by shelling residential neighbourhoods. Hussein then turned his attention north to Kurdistan where the Kurds, inspired by the rebels in the south, had launched their own rebellion. Again, the Kurdish rebellion collapsed in the face of the vastly superior Iraqi firepower and lack of US support.

Human rights groups put the Kurdish death toll at around 100,000.

As part of the formal ceasefire agreement, Iraq agreed to destroy its entire chemical and biological weapons inventory, disassemble its nuclear weapons program, and submit to UN weapons inspectors, who found evidence that Hussein's nuclear weapons program was much more advanced than had been previously thought. As well, facing an international outcry over the plight of the Kurds, the Allies eventually moved to carve out safe havens in northern and southern Iraq, protected by US and UK fighter jets. Hussein periodically engineered crises—threatening coalition planes in the no-fly zones, moving troops within striking distance of Kuwait, hampering inspectors, or meddling with the Kurds. This brought intermittent US and British bombing raids for the twelve years leading up to the 2003 conflict.

Under the insistence of the US, the UN imposed a harsh sanctions regime on Iraq that could only be lifted if the country were disarmed of its weapons of mass destruction and accepted unimpeded inspections. UN humanitarian agencies blame the sanctions for hundreds of thousands of premature deaths in Iraq. At the same time, sanctions gave Hussein a convenient external scapegoat for the suffering of Iraqis. His grip on power was hardly affected by the embargo, and Hussein earned enough income by smuggling oil through Iraq's willing neighbours—often with the West's acquiescence—to buy his military's loyalty.

Iraqi co-operation with the UN did not last long. Throughout the period between the 1991 and 2003 wars, Hussein played a game with his US and UK minders, hoping to weaken their political will and increase Arab sympathy for Iraq to the point where the regime could break out of its isolation. In 1993, coalition forces conducted two limited air strikes against Iraq, once for refusing to remove missiles from southern Iraq and once in retaliation for a plot to assassinate former President George H. Bush. In 1997, Iraq tried to bar Americans from the UN inspection teams, and in 1998 Iraq declared that presidential palaces were off-limits to inspectors. Although it backed down under the threat of force, UN inspectors reported that the Iraqis were still not complying. This led to the withdrawal of inspectors and the launching of Desert Fox, a four-day United States and British bombing campaign.

Iraqi compliance only resumed after September 11, when US President George W. Bush included Iraq in an "axis of evil," and began threatening the use of force. On November 8, 2002, the UN Security Council unanimously adopted Resolution 1441, requiring Iraq to allow weapons inspectors back in or face "serious consequences." Caught off guard, Iraq suddenly announced it would readmit weapons inspectors after an absence of four years.

The war against Iraq began when the US, with the UK at its side, decided it would wait no longer for the UN inspection process to conclude that there were no weapons of mass destruction in Iraq. President Bush told the American people: "The UN Security Council has not lived up to its responsibilities." That statement—the ultimate justification for going to war—could not have been more wrong. Only days before, the chief UN inspectors, Hans Blix and Mohammed elBaradei, had told the Security Council that the inspection process was working. Destruction of all Iraq's Al Samoud 2 missiles, well along when war broke out, was described by Blix as "a very significant piece of disarmament." elBaradei said: "After three months of intensive inspections, we have to date found no evidence of a nuclear weapons programme in Iraq." The two inspectors said their findings were based on the work of 84 inspectors who had conducted 500 inspections of 350 sites. Despite the fact that professional inspectors could not find anything even remotely giving Iraq the power to launch an attack using weapons of mass destruction, the US struck on March 19, 2003.

Having at first said that the disarmament of Iraq was its chief concern, the Bush Administration shifted the reason for war to "regime change," then to stimulating democracy throughout the Middle East, and then to the liberation of the Iraqi people. This continually changing line of reasoning made many countries skeptical of the US position. The lack of evidence that the inspection process was not working, combined with the shifting motivation for attack, was responsible for the diplomatic setback the US received at the UN Security Council. This debacle at the UN was caused not only by France's threatened veto of a resolution to authorize war, but also by the reluctance of the six smaller states on the Council—Mexico, Chile, Pakistan, Guinea, Cameroon, and Angola—to vote for such a resolution. The diplomatic setback for the US was made worse when its closest neighbours, Canada and Mexico, refused to participate in the US-led coalition.

Almost overnight, the strategy of containment—which had worked well for the US against the Soviet Union during the long years of the Cold War—was abandoned. Over the past decade, the strategy of containing Iraq had destroyed more weapons than in the Gulf War, dismantled Iraq's nuclear weapons program, and halted its medium- and long-range missile programs. Nonetheless, the new US doctrine of pre-emptive attack was invoked. This act aroused the ire of people around the world, particularly in Islamic countries. The war against Saddam was seen by many in the Arab world as a war against Islam. The authority of the UN was clearly undermined by the US and UK challenge.

This resentment against the US goes far beyond the Iraq crisis. The combination of unprecedented US military strength with an aggressive foreign policy centring on the new doctrine of pre-emptive attack has struck fear and anger into nations around the world. Through its rejection of the Anti-Ballistic Missile Treaty, the Comprehensive Test Ban Treaty, the Anti-Personnel Landmines Treaty, the International

Criminal Court, and the Kyoto Protocol on the environment, the US is seen as not respecting the multilateral processes of international law. It is regarded as a "hyperpower" using its military strength for dominance. The week the Iraq war began, *Newsweek* magazine ran a cover article, "Why America Scares the World," which said, "Never have so many of its allies been so firmly opposed to its policies. Never has it provoked as much public opposition, resentment and mistrust. And all this before the first shot has been fired."

When the US turned its back on the UN in launching the attack, it violated the UN Charter, which does not permit military action without an attack or the imminent threat of one. American and British leaders claimed that their actions in attacking Iraq and removing Saddam Hussein from power were just. But nothing was said of the morality of removing an inspection process that was working, or of the "collateral damage" to civilians, or of the humanitarian crises caused by the war. The war was not legal, since it was not authorized by the UN and was not fought in self-defence. Hans Blix was justly furious. In a scathing attack on the US and the UK, he accused them of planning the war "well in advance," and of "fabricating" evidence against Iraq to justify their campaign.

As the months went by following the Iraq war with no weapons of mass destruction being found, the truthfulness of the US and the UK administrations was increasingly challenged. The resistance encountered by the allied military forces belied the pre-war claims that they would be welcomed. War can hardly be said to have settled "the Iraq problem."

Neither can the attack on Iraq be considered a "just war." It was not a last resort, did not possess legitimate authority, and certainly did not spare civilians. This was pointed out by Pope John Paul II and many other religious leaders, and also by a number of political leaders, not least among them former US President Jimmy Carter.

Both the Afghan and Iraq wars expose the problems with the "just war" concept in today's world. The prosecutors of the wars claimed it was a just act to bomb to root out terrorists, in the case of Afghanistan, and to decapitate the Iraq regime, in the case of Iraq. A gullible public, shocked by the outrages of the World Trade Center and the Pentagon terrorist attacks and manipulated by government propaganda, gave its support, though the support was far from total. The extent of the protests showed that war itself is finally being challenged as a means of resolving conflict.

"Just War" Theory Is Outmoded

The just war tradition is as old as warfare itself. Early records of collective fighting indicate that some moral considerations were used by warriors. They may have involved sparing women and children and the treatment of prisoners. While parts of the Bible hint at ethical behaviour in war and concepts of a just cause, the most systematic study is provided by St. Thomas Aquinas. In the *Summa Theologica,* he presents the general outline of what became known as the just war theory. He discusses not only the justification of war, but also the kinds of activity that are permissible in war. The work of Hugo Grotius (1583–1645), generally considered to be the father of international law, can be traced back to Aquinas.

Just war theory offers a series of principles that aim to retain a plausible moral framework for war. Both the justice of war (*jus ad bellum*) and the conduct of war (*jus in bello*) are considered. The principles of the justice of war are commonly held to be having a just cause, being declared by a proper authority, possessing right intention, having a reasonable chance of success, and the end being proportional to the means used. Possessing a just cause is often considered the most important condition. Self-defence against aggression is considered a just cause.

The rules of just conduct of war fall under the two broad principles of discrimination and proportionality. In waging war, it is considered unfair and unjust to attack indiscriminately, since non-combatants or innocents are deemed to stand outside the field of war proper. Also, any act of war should remain strictly proportional to the objective desired. Proportionality requires tempering the extent and violence of warfare to minimize destruction and casualties. Thus the principles of proportionality and discrimination aim to temper war's violence and scope.

To say that the just war criteria have been honoured more in the breach than the observance in the conflicts of the past century is to state the obvious. While there have been international agreements for the protection of prisoners of war, the conduct of war generally has made a mockery of the rules for a just war. Examples of the savagery of the prosecutors of war, even in these so-called modern times, include the carpet bombing of cities during World War II, the killing of whole villages in Vietnam, the use of biological and chemical agents, and the systematic use of rape as a weapon. Other such examples are the destruction of infrastructures so that survivors of conflict would have no water or food; the Holocaust; and the mass killings of innocents in Cambodia, Rwanda, and elsewhere. Every kind of weapon ever invented has been used and the number of innocent people killed with these weapons greatly exceeds the number of combatants.

The moral teaching derived from the just war principles has been strong. For example, the Second Vatican Council (1962–65) taught:

> Any act of war aimed indiscriminately at the destruction of entire cities or of extensive areas along with their population is a crime against God and man himself. It merits unequivocal and unhesitating condemnation.

The Council, conceding that war has not yet been rooted out of human affairs, said that as long as the danger of war remains and there is no competent and sufficiently powerful authority at the international level, "governments cannot be denied the right to legitimate defence once every means of peaceful settlement has been exhausted." But they insisted that the possession of war material does not make every military or political use of it lawful. And then this warning:

> ... the arms race is an utterly treacherous trap for humanity, and one which injures the poor to an intolerable degree. It is much to be feared that if this race persists, it will eventually spawn all the lethal ruin whose path it is now making ready.

In this moral teaching, legitimate self-defence is allowed "once every means of peaceful settlement has been exhausted." A state does not have the right to automatically respond to an attack with military action. War is only allowed as a last resort for self-defence. Similarly, the UN Charter does not give a state blanket authorization for war in self-defence. Under Article 51, any action taken in the right of self-defence must be reported to the Security Council, which has the primary authority to maintain or restore international peace and security. The aggrieved nation must then act only under the mandate of the Security Council.

It is the existence of the Security Council that forces us to review the just war theory. Only the Security Council can authorize war. No state by itself, or even with a "coalition of the willing," can any longer invoke the just war theory as a cover for self-interested military actions.

Two main developments in recent history have eroded much of the validity that just war principles had in past times. First, for a very long time, when states or sub-groups quarrelled, no legitimate supra-national body had authority to resolve the dispute or mediate a resolution. Lacking some greater authority, they simply went to war. The League of Nations, which came into being after World War I, was impotent from the start. But when the UN was established after World War II, the world suddenly had new machinery to keep the peace. The UN gave its Security Council the authority to maintain international peace and security by investigating and recommending solutions to disputes, applying economic sanctions against an aggressor, and taking military action against the belligerent if all else failed.

The veto power possessed by each of the five permanent members of the Security Council (the US, Russia, the UK, France, and China) keeps the Security Council from enforcing its resolutions; the major powers will not let it have a standing force capable of rapid deployment to zones of conflict. For example, when Resolution 1267 was adopted in 1999 calling for Afghanistan to surrender Osama bin Laden, the UN was unable to enforce its directive. Also, when Iraq invaded Kuwait in 1990, Kuwait could not quickly appeal to a UN force to stop the invasion. It is very doubtful that Saddam Hussein would have risked losing Arab support by crossing a UN-protected border. In both instances, Afghanistan and the Persian Gulf War, the US invoked the just war principle of a just cause and legitimate authority. If the UN had been properly used, war could have been avoided.

War has been averted and mediated in many instances where the UN's mediation and arbitration role was respected. Angola, El Salvador, Mozambique, Guatemala, Namibia, and Cambodia are but a few examples. If the UN legal machinery is deliberately kept weak, then the very states that are keeping it weak cannot legitimately claim a just right to make war when there is a crisis. However, if states are determined to have a war, they will. At least, with the international machinery of peaceful resolution available, states can no longer legitimately claim to wage a just war on their own.

Second, the just war principles of discrimination and proportionality in the conduct of war have been completely outmoded by the development of weapons of mass destruction. When wars were fought by soldiers more or less in hand-to-hand combat, there was some chance that only enemy soldiers would be engaged. But regional conflicts today involve close-in fighting, where wars extend into the local populace; the destruction of the environment and the use of rape and torture as weapons of war scar the lives of innocent people. When air raids with conventional bombs began, civilians came under direct attack even if they were not the intended target. Since the military and economic assets of a country are usually maintained in urban or semi-urban areas, it is impossible to bomb a military establishment without affecting the local populace. This is why the bombing raids of both the Allied and the Axis powers during World War II resulted in unprecedented civilian casualties.

When precision munitions were invented, it was claimed that they could be guided from far away to within meters of the intended military target. This may be so in theory, but the number of civilian casualties from missiles that went astray in modern conflicts proves their fallibility. The atomic bombs dropped on Hiroshima and Nagasaki were totally lacking in any sense of discrimination and proportionality. Civilians far from the epicentre of both attacks died horrible deaths from burning and radiation, and many continue to live with the long-term effects. The development and refinement of nuclear and other weapons of mass destruction have only increased these weapons' destructive capacity, and have brought the potential for warfare to every corner of the globe.

The just war concept, as it has been invoked by a single state in the past, has been stripped of much credibility by modern developments. The only way it can legitimately be invoked today is through the UN Security Council's application of Articles 41 and 42. Article 41 allows the Council, when it has decided there is a breach of the peace, to invoke economic sanctions against an aggressor. Article 42 states that if sanctions prove inadequate, "it may take such action by air, sea, or land forces as may be necessary to maintain or restore international peace and security." The military forces of members of the UN may then be used. Indeed, under Article 45, member states are to make military units available "for combined international enforcement action." The Military Staff Committee of the UN, composed of high-ranking military officers from the permanent members of the Security Council, is supposed to oversee such operations. But the permanent members have never been able to agree on what kind of power it should have, and the committee is dysfunctional.

Here, the work of the International Commission on Intervention and State Sovereignty has been very helpful in defining the conditions under which military action can be taken to avert a humanitarian disaster. The Commission's report, "The Responsibility to Protect," sets the just cause threshold very high, and requires that civilians be faced with serious harm, either through large-scale loss of life or through ethnic cleansing, before a military intervention may proceed. Even then, the Commission sees the UN Security Council as the principal authority sanctioning force. Nonetheless, as I have argued above, the failure to use the existing machinery for peace properly does not confer on a state the right to claim its wars are automatically just.

The record speaks for itself. Overwhelmingly, the victims of modern wars are innocent civilians. Limitation and proportionality, the chief criteria of humanitarian law, have become a fiction. It is impossible to contain the effects of weapons of mass destruction to a military objective. The violence and range of war are no longer tempered. Also, the claim that serious disputes cannot be resolved without warfare rings hollow in the modern age, which has at its disposal a wide array of UN tools. If states will not put themselves under the purview of the UN in resolving conflict, that is a sad reflection of their own obduracy. But at least they should be deprived of any legitimacy by the international community in claiming their war is "just." We still live in a period of political ambiguity. The logic of just war has been superseded by the scientific, cultural, and legal developments of the modern world. But politically, society lags behind, burdened by the trappings of the culture of war.

2

The Effect of Militarism on a Fragile Planet

The Earth Summit in Rio de Janeiro in 1992, billed as the largest demonstration of global diplomacy ever attempted, showed the difficulties of moving out of the war mentality. The world conference, which brought together the leaders of 178 countries, fused the two key issues of the environment and development, and produced Agenda 21, a detailed blueprint of 115 programs to address the many strands of sustainable development. The estimated cost of implementing Agenda 21 was $625 billion. For their part, the developing countries agreed to pay $500 billion, leaving only $125 billion to be paid by the developed countries. This request was immediately rejected as being outrageously high, yet it was no more than the UN's Official Development Assistance target of 0.7 per cent of gross national product (GNP) that developed countries agreed to pay in 1969. New aid announced at Rio did not amount to much more than $2 billion. That same year, the developed countries spent $584 billion on their militaries. When the 2003 UN Human Development Report was published, evidence showed that 54 least developed countries are worse off than a decade earlier.

The Rio Summit took place in a climate of optimism. The polarization of East–West relations had ended, the UN was working more successfully, there were hopes that global problems could be managed. The Summit tackled the sustainable development needs of the twenty-first century. Detailed programs at the local, regional, and international levels addressed issues including:

- Protecting the atmosphere and the oceans

- Combating deforestation, desertification, and drought

- Dealing with indigenous peoples and women and their roles in implementing sustainable development

- Meeting basic human needs such as health, education, and housing

- Eradicating poverty

- Making the transition to patterns of production and consumption in the industrialized countries to significantly reduce pollution.

In effect, a new global partnership was envisaged to build a more efficient and equitable world economy. If sufficient money for sustainable development could not be raised at this moment, when could it?

While some elements of Agenda 21 have been advanced, Rio is mostly noted as a lost opportunity. Ten years later, in 2002, government leaders reassembled in Johannesburg to review their progress. The report card on Rio's accomplishments was dismal. Despite Agenda 21, the environment had continued to deteriorate, poverty had increased, and the number of armed conflicts had risen. A group of Nobel Peace Laureates and mayors of large cities, headed by former President of the Soviet Union Mikhail Gorbachev, who now leads a foundation devoted to world peace issues, released a devastating assessment of life on the planet at the time of the Johannesburg Summit:

- 1.2 billion people live on less than $1 a day.

- 800 million people are suffering from hunger.

- 1.1 billion human beings do not have access to safe drinking water.

- 2.4 billion people lack adequate sanitation services.

- 5 million individuals, predominantly women and children, die every year from diseases related to water quality.

- 2 billion people do not have access to electricity.

- 25 million refugees have fled their homes for environmental reasons.

- The standard of living of the average African family has decreased by 20 per cent in the past ten years.

- 36 million human beings are infected with HIV/AIDS; 23 million of these live in Africa and have no access to any treatment.

- Developing countries lose $100 billion a year due to imbalances and unjust trade tariffs imposed by developed countries.

- The average level of Official Development Assistance from developed countries is only 0.22 per cent of gross national product [GNP], far short of the UN target of 0.7 per cent.

- The urban population of 2.5 billion will increase to 5 billion in the next 25 years, putting perilous stress on social services.

- 12 per cent of the 1.7 million known species of plants and animals are threatened with extinction.

- Average world temperatures are projected to increase, by 1.2° to 3.5°C (2° to 6°F), over the course of the twenty-first century. This could exacerbate flooding, fires, and other natural disasters across the world; melt glaciers and the polar ice caps; raise sea levels; and pose threats to hundreds of millions of coastal and island dwellers.

This distinguished group of Nobel Laureates and mayors declared that the planet was "in danger." They further accused governments, and their self-interested "business as usual" policies, of creating a social, economic, and ecological impasse for the six billion inhabitants of the planet. These policies are also seen as compromising the survival of the 5 to 6 billion additional people who will populate the Earth by the end of the century.

The Johannesburg Summit addressed five main action areas.

1) For water and sanitation, governments made a commitment to reduce by half the number of people without access to safe drinking water and sanitation by 2015.

2) For energy, governments pledged to increase access to modern energy services, particularly in Africa.

3) For health, governments agreed that chemicals should not be used in ways that harm human health, and they further agreed on more co-operation to reduce air pollution.

4) For agriculture, they established food security strategies for Africa to be implemented by 2005.

5) For the environment, they made commitments to reduce biodiversity loss, to restore fisheries, and to protect the marine environment.

A number of partnerships were formed between governments and the private sector to move ahead on these five goals. There was a good deal of discussion about opening up access to markets for developing countries, phasing out export subsidies, and promoting corporate responsibility and accountability.

But in the end, less than $3 billion in new money was pledged for the Global Environment Facility, the main instrument for implementing the Johannesburg targets. While it would be wrong to say that the Johannesburg Summit was not worth the effort and money spent on it, the fact is that it accomplished little in relation to the magnitude of the problems it addressed. Time frames were set on only three issues: improving sanitation, restoring depleted fish stocks, and reducing the rate of extinction of the world's plants and animals. Goals on issues such as drinking water, biodiversity, chemicals, and Official Development Assistance were either weakly reaffirmed or deleted. In fact, much of the text in the final document merely reiterated previous commitments, and was a far cry from accepting responsibility. UN Secretary-General Kofi Annan had urged delegates to take "responsibility for each other —but especially the poor, the vulnerable, and the oppressed—as fellow members of a single human family."

Disarmament and Development: A Critical Relationship

What is holding back humanity from achieving equitable development for all the world's peoples? It is certainly not a shortage of capital. In 2001, world economic output totalled $31.5 trillion—triple the economic output of the 1960s. In the past half century, world population has more than doubled. That is a sizable growth in demand for the basics of life, but world economic growth could easily have taken care of basic human needs. Nor is there a shortage of resources—oil, natural gas, nuclear power, water, food, and housing materials—if evenly applied. But there is a severe shortage of political will in the Western countries to ensure that every human being has access to the four pillars of human security: peace, development, equity, and justice. The Nobel Laureates were right in saying the "self-interested policies of business as usual" are the causes of an unsustainable future.

In a damning criticism of rich Western countries, Prime Minister Dato Seri Mahathir Mohamed of Malaysia addressed the opening of the 2003 Summit of the Non Aligned Movement (NAM). The NAM, composed of 116 developing countries, was founded in 1961 to promote the interests of the South in economic and political issues. Mahathir, who has headed the Malaysian government since 1981, chaired the movement in 2003. He excoriated capitalist free traders whose "greed knows no bounds," and rogue currency traders, who had "destroyed the economies of half the world."

> Now the rich give no more aid. They do not lend either. And all the time, the international agencies they control try to strangle the debt-laden poor countries which had been attacked by their greedy market manipulators. ... The rich want to squeeze out literally the last drop of blood from the poor.

This confrontation between the haves and have-nots, the developed and the developing, has produced a world that is practically ungovernable, he said.

> Since September 11, 2001, the rich and the powerful have become enraged with the poor half of the world. And their extreme measures to ensure security for themselves have only amplified the anger of the oppressed poor. Both sides are now in a state of blind anger and are bent on killing each other, on war.

Acknowledging that outlawing war is a daunting task, he said:

> Unless we take the moral high ground now, we will wait in vain for the powerful North to voluntarily give up slaughtering people in the name of national interest.

This indictment of the West was, not surprisingly, mostly ignored by the Western media. Mahathir's withering criticism is undoubtedly unpalatable for many, if not most, in the West. But we need to hear it. It contains a basic truth—and it is a warning that if the gulf between the two worlds is not bridged, turbulence and ever more violent storms lie ahead.

For the most part, governments and financial institutions exclude many of those they seek to govern, especially women, indigenous people, and the poor. They are heavily influenced by the demands of the rich, usually the corporate rich who have a mentality that seeks to preserve and expand their wealth—wealth built on power. And power is built on militarism. There is no clearer example of this than that of the five permanent members of the Security Council. The very nations charged with maintaining peace and security and upholding the values of the UN Charter maintain the world's biggest armies, account for the lion's share of world military expenditures, hold virtually all nuclear weapons, are the biggest arms merchants, and dominate the world economy. They quite literally run the world. And they use the war culture to maintain their power.

Are the permanent members responsible for all of the world's ills? Of course not. The greed and corruption, the misguided policies, and the totalitarianism found in so many countries around the world also share in the responsibility for this dilemma. Many developing countries spend at least as much on arms as on health and education. Also, the growing populations need more energy and resources, which leads to more pollution. Just as there is no one single solution to all problems, there is no one identifiable cause. But there is a dominant characteristic: the legitimate aspirations of humanity are constantly being dashed by power structures underpinned by a war culture.

In 1987, the UN, concerned that the costs of war were siphoning off money needed for the development of peoples, convened an International Conference on the Relationship Between Disarmament and Development. It emphasized that the military absorption of the world's human, financial, natural, and technological resources affects the international flow of trade, finance, and technology in addition to hindering the process of confidence-building among states. Global military expenditures are in dramatic contrast to what is spent on economic and social development and relate to the misery and poverty afflicting two-thirds of humanity. The final report concluded:

> The world can either continue to pursue the arms race with characteristic vigour or move consciously and with deliberate speed toward a more stable and balanced social

and economic development within a more sustainable international economic and political order; it cannot do both.

This conference opened the door to a new definition of security. The development and production of weapons had always been justified by the perceived need to protect the security of the state. The conference acknowledged that security is an overriding priority for all nations. But it also counterbalanced this with the recognition that security in the new interdependent age of planet-threatening technologies demands both disarmament and development:

> Security consists of not only military, but also political, economic, social, humanitarian and human rights and ecological aspects.

Though the benefits to humanity from diverting a portion of military spending to economic and social development are clear, governments have backed away from implementing the conclusions of the Disarmament and Development Conference. The US refused to attend the conference, claiming that no such relationship exists. This has had a chilling effect on other developed countries. The global conferences of the 1990s have paid only perfunctory attention to the linkage of disarmament and development.

The 1995 UN World Social Summit's final document contained only a brief reference, noting the "negative impact on development of excessive military expenditures, the arms trade, and investment for arms production." In the run-up to this special meeting, the UN Human Development Report suggested that the Summit was an ideal opportunity for nations to endorse the principle that no nation should spend more on its military than on the education and health of its people. It suggested that nations should also agree to a 3 per cent reduction in military spending over the next decade, with the money saved going to a global fund for human security. None of these measures was advanced at the

Summit. At the previous Rio Summit, military issues were conspicuously absent from any of the documentation, even those sections dealing with radioactive wastes and toxic chemicals.

Ten years later, the Johannesburg Summit missed an extraordinary opportunity to address the same issue. Though this Summit's final document referred to peace and security as "essential" for sustainable development, it took no account of the $850 billion the world was spending that year on its militaries. Each of the UN conferences has struggled to find a consensus for its action plan. The exclusion of references to arms spending is largely due to the blocking tactics of a few militarily powerful countries, which oppose any attempts to raise these issues. Since the major powers are hostile to any suggestion that their military spending deprives the poor, the issue is continually glossed over.

In rejecting a peace dividend for the poor, the powerful countries are laying the groundwork for more instability and chaos in the years ahead. The persistence of a culture of war results in countries being preoccupied with their own security. They should, instead, be focused on how to prevent a class struggle of unprecedented violence in the future between the world's poorest and richest people. September 11 may well prove to be a foreshadowing of this violent struggle.

This diversion of resources toward militarism results in a lost opportunity for sustainable development. World military research alone totals $58 billion per year. Of the 2.25 million scientists involved in research worldwide, about 500,000 work in a military capacity. Of physicists and engineers, 50 per cent work exclusively on the development of weapons. A single nuclear submarine costs as much as the annual education budgets of the 23 least developed countries, who have 160 million school-age children. Sending every child in the world to school would cost only $7 billion. The world spends this amount in military expenditures every three days.

It is ironic that the war culture, draining world resources that are so badly needed to implement sustainable development (which would alleviate sources of conflict in the future), is itself a reason why conflicts will grow. Defensive militarism produces war, not peace. All the world systems that sustain life are under heavy strain. The seeds of future, and far more calamitous, conflicts are being widely sown today.

Military Impact on the Environment

The effect of militarism plays out on the planet's ecosystems in many ways—both directly and indirectly. This subject is a neglected aspect of the sustainable development debate. The culture of war affects the physical environment in five significant ways:

1) **Pollution of the air, land, and water in peacetime**. The world's military forces are responsible for the release of more than two-thirds of CFC-113, an ozone-depleting chemical. As a result of naval accidents, at least 50 nuclear warheads and 11 nuclear reactors litter the ocean floor. The Pentagon generates five times more toxins than the five major US chemical companies combined and is the largest single source of US environmental pollution. The cost of cleaning up military-related sites in the US alone is estimated to be upwards of $500 billion.

2) **Immediate and long-term impacts of armed conflict**. Stresses on the environment and human safety have been caused by radiation from nuclear explosions (Hiroshima, Nagasaki); agricultural perils caused by land mines (many African and Asian countries) and unexploded remnants of war (Kosovo, Afghanistan); chemical agents and burning of oil wells (Gulf War).

Retreating armies have long used scorched-earth tactics to lay waste to enemy territories. Historical examples include Napoleon's retreat from Moscow and the Nazis in the Soviet

Union and northern Norway. "Agent Orange" and other US defoliants were used during the Vietnam War, which rendered about a third of Vietnam a wasteland. The ecological devastation of the country will take generations to repair.

In the Gulf War of 1991, oil wells were ignited and four to eight million barrels of oil were spilled into the sea, severely damaging 460 miles of coastline. The fuel-air bombs used to clear minefields pulverized topsoil and destroyed all nearby vegetation. Use of ammunition with depleted uranium has led to longer-term radiation effects, including birth defects in Iraq and are a possible factor behind Gulf War Syndrome. The coalition forces left huge quantities of refuse, toxic materials, and 50 million gallons of sewage in sand pits.

During the NATO military action in Kosovo and the former Federal Republic of Yugoslavia, air attacks resulted in severe environmental damage. Burning oil refineries leaked oil products and chemicals into the Danube River. Chemical plants were bombed, spreading extremely dangerous substances into the air.

3) **Militarization of Outer Space.** Outer space is already militarized with missile systems dependent on guidance from satellites. The US missile defence program now underway will step up this process. If introduced into space, the danger of contamination through conventional or nuclear explosives will be significant.

4) **Nuclear Weapons Development and Production.** Radioactive fallout from now banned atmospheric nuclear tests is estimated to have caused as many as 86,000 birth defects and 150,000 premature deaths, and it may eventually result in some two million cancer deaths. Uranium mining, conducted in many countries, is known to lead to severe cases of contamination. Russia's surplus stocks of chemical, biological, and nuclear weapons present such a serious environmental and security challenge that the G8, following their 2002 meeting, set up a special fund to clean up the debris.

5) **Land use.** People around the world have been displaced where the military takes land from local residents for use as bases, target ranges, weapons stores, and training grounds. Examples include Thule, Greenland, where indigenous Inuit were displaced for a US base, and the US bases in Okinawa, Guantanamo, and Diego Garcia. Military activities often involve the use of fuels, explosives, and toxic substances. When improperly handled or stored, they can seep into the environment and affect nearby communities. Military exercises often damage farmland, as heavy vehicles travel over small roads and bridges. In the lands of the Innu in Canada, noise pollution from low-flying military aircraft has proved a serious menace, and has even affected the rearing of animals.

Food and Water: Basic Elements

Inseparable from concern for the environment is secure access to safe water and the ability to produce adequate food for all. World population passed 6 billion in 2000, up from 4.4 billion in 1980, and 2.5 billion in 1950. The population is expected to grow to about 8 billion in 2025, to close to 9 billion in 2050, and eventually to stabilize between 10.5 and 11 billion. Thus the world will need to feed, house, and support about 5 billion additional people. Virtually all future population growth will occur in the developing world. This increased population, combined with higher standards of living, particularly in the developing countries, will pose enormous strains on land, water, energy, and other natural resources. The most basic elements required for human existence are food and water. Yet millions die every year because they do not have reliable access to either. Hunger and unsafe water are among the top health risks in the world.

The UN Food and Agriculture Organization (FAO) reported in 2002 that 840 million people worldwide are undernourished and, of these, millions died from hunger, including 6 million children under the age of five. In 2003, when it became clear that the international community was distracted from African famine by the Middle East crises, the UN World Food Programme (WFP) joined the FAO in appealing urgently for food aid to keep 15 million people from facing starvation in East and West Africa. In the war-torn Central African Republic, famine threatens one million. "This can be called the world's most silent crisis, a drama that is being played out amid total indifference, a civil war tearing apart a country without anyone talking about it," said Christiane Berthiaume, a spokesperson for the WFP.

Famine stunts the development of people, saps their strength and cripples their immune system. In the worst affected countries, a newborn child has a life expectancy of 38 years, compared to more than 70 in wealthier nations. One in seven children born into countries where hunger is most common will die before reaching the age of five. More than two billion people suffer from micro nutrient malnutrition: their diets supply inadequate amounts of vitamins and minerals such as Vitamins A and C, iron, iodine, and zinc, which are all essential nutrients for human growth and development. Children and women are most vulnerable. Between 100 and 140 million children suffer from Vitamin A deficiency, which can lead to blindness. Some 20 million people are mentally handicapped as a result of iodine deficiency. The World Health Organization has observed that poor countries today have 170 million underweight children, more than three million of whom die each year, and contrasts this to the one billion people in the world who are overweight and at least 300 million who are clinically obese. The contrast between the haves and have-nots could not be more starkly illustrated.

"We do not have the excuse that we cannot grow enough food or that we do not know enough about how to eliminate hunger," Dr. Jacques Diouf, FAO Director-General, said. "What remains to be proven is that we care enough, that our expressions of concern in international forums are more than rhetoric, that we will no longer accept and ignore the suffering of hungry people or the daily death toll of 25,000 victims of hunger and poverty." Conflict is one of the most common causes of food insecurity. War and civil strife were the major causes of food emergencies in fifteen countries in 2001 and 2002. The overall impact of armed conflicts on food security disrupts food production and economic activity by displacing rural populations within a country and across borders. At the household level, the displaced are no longer able to produce for themselves or their families and therefore become totally dependent on food assistance or become malnourished and eventually die of starvation or diseases related to malnutrition. At the national level, scarce resources in a poor country are diverted to the conflict (armaments, expanded armies, and so forth), leaving the country unable to import food to meet basic requirements. The country, therefore, becomes dependent on food aid.

Armed conflicts displace people from their homes or trap them in combat zones and make them dependent on temporary food assistance. In 2001, the number of displaced people was estimated at 37 million (12 million refugees and 25 million internally displaced people). In conflict situations, food sources and supplies may be intentionally disrupted by opposing groups as a means of starving civilians. In 1999, such disruptions left close to 24 million people hungry and in need of humanitarian assistance. Armed conflict may prevent farmers from producing food and disrupt transport, trade, and markets, thereby reducing access to food. The FAO has found that conflict-induced losses of agricultural output in sub-Saharan Africa between 1970 and 1997 were equivalent to 75 per cent of all aid received by conflict-affected countries.

Fresh water, the foremost requirement for life, is becoming scarce and will be the source of increasing conflicts in the future. According to the 2003 UN World Water

Development Report, 1.1 billion people across the globe lack enough safe water to meet minimum requirements. A total of 2.4 billion do not have decent sanitation. What these statistics mean is that in the slums of Dhaka, Bangladesh, the majority of the people use buckets or pits in the ground for toilets. In the Kibera slum of Nairobi, 200 people share each pit latrine. Contaminated water causes dysentery and other chronic gastrointestinal diseases; in 2000 the estimated number of deaths from this scourge—which could be easily controlled if governments gave a priority to clean water—was 2,213,000. Coverage of this story and these deaths is rare in Western media. Yet when seven people in the Ontario farming community of Walkerton died from drinking water infected by E. coli, it became a national scandal in Canada.

Water tables are now falling on every continent, and many countries are facing water shortages as 80 million additional people stake their claims to the earth's water resources each year. Although 70 per cent of the earth's surface is covered with salt water, the global supply of fresh water is severely limited. As populations increase, irrigation of essential food crops will use more water. Agriculture is competing with industrial, household, and environmental uses of water. As these demands increase, groundwater is being depleted and other water ecosystems are becoming polluted and degraded. Already, serious questions are arising as to whether there will be enough water to grow food for the eight billion people who are expected to populate the earth by 2025.

The developing world will pay the highest price for the water crisis, since this is where food production increases are most needed and where water shortages are most acute. Scarcities are already evident in the Middle East and Southwest Asia. According to the World Bank, eleven countries—Algeria, Egypt, Israel, Jordan, Libya, Morocco, Saudi Arabia, Syria, Tunisia, the United Arab Emirates, and Yemen—have barely enough water to meet current minimum needs. The major shared water systems of these areas—the Nile, the Jordan, the Tigris–Euphrates, and the Indus—have been the sites of human conflict throughout history.

The Nile, the longest river in the world, stretching from equatorial Africa to the Mediterranean Sea, is a particular flashpoint. If the combined population of the three countries through which the Nile runs—Ethiopia, Sudan, and Egypt—rises as predicted from 150 million today to 340 million in 2050, competition for the limited water resources could be intense. The great bulk of the Nile is used by Egypt, which would certainly fight off any challenge to its access. In fact, Egypt has long used military force to maintain control over the Nile headwaters. In the dying years of the previous Ethiopian government, tensions with Egypt increased rapidly when the rulers in Addis Ababa, Ethiopia, pondered the construction of dams on the Nile. Another potential water war exists in Southern Africa; this would involve Botswana, Namibia, and Angola.

The implications of water scarcity are far-reaching. Investment commitments from national governments, international donors, and development banks are weak because military spending claims too high a proportion of discretionary spending. A developing water crisis will lead to a breakdown in domestic water service for hundreds of millions of people, devastating loss of wetlands, serious reductions in food production, and skyrocketing food prices that would force declining per capita food production in much of the world.

Present trends indicate that by 2025, nearly half the world's population—some 3.5 billion people—will live in areas facing serious water shortages. Since the demand for water will grow while the supply will not, the conditions for conflict are likely to escalate. Michael T. Klare, author of *Resource Wars: The New Landscape of Global Conflict*, says it is not hard to imagine the kinds of clashes these food and water shortages will produce:

Greatly contributing to the risk of conflict is the close relationship between internal and external security. The leaders of these countries are expected to provide the basic necessities of human life, especially water and food; if they fail in this, they lose their mandate to rule and can expect rising political unrest. In such circumstances, leaders usually respond in one of two ways: they attempt to stifle internal dissent through repressive measures, or they try to channel the discontent against external enemies, who are held responsible for the deprivation. The first approach can lead to civil war; the second, to interstate conflict.

Averting a water crisis that could escalate into conflict requires a mix of water policy and management reforms, and investments tailored to specific countries and basins— solutions that require political commitment and money. Without this commitment, in just 20 years there will not be enough water for cities, households, the environment, or agriculture.

When the Cold War ended, there was brief talk of a peace dividend for humanity. This has not happened. Not even the fundamental issues of water and food have been satisfactorily resolved. The inexorable pressure of the military–industrial complex has kept military expenditures high in most parts of the world, both rich and poor. And, since September 11, armed forces are demanding, and receiving, more money. Many civil society groups call for increased funding for sustainable development, but governments do not hear their voices. Governments are so trapped in a weapon-based security syndrome that they have forgotten how disarmament serves development goals. During the Johannesburg Summit, a parallel Global People's Forum was held. Attending this Forum were representatives of women, youth, labour, indigenous peoples, farmers, NGOs, and others—including disabled people, the elderly, and social movements. Their statement said the current military spending decreases chances for sustainable development and does nothing to address the economic injustices that often lie at the root of conflict:

> The massive spending on armaments and war must be diverted to sustainable development initiatives. Attacks to gain access to resources must be declared as a crime on humanity.

Their call for spending on equitable economic and social development ran up against the wasteful behaviour of the rich and the desperate practices of the very poor, which strain the ecosystem. A strong private sector presence at Johannesburg emphasized trade gains rather than equitable development. The trend toward the privatization, or commodification, of clean water was a sore point for many. It seemed clear that asking private firms to arrange access to water was not an effective way to get it to poor people. The weak measures to limit fossil fuel emissions were also seen to exacerbate inequality, with the poor being in the most polluted parts of cities and on marginal lands. The representative of St. Lucia, who spoke for the small island states, said his country had set a high standard to replace fossil fuel with renewable energy, but that "the World Bank asks us to privatize our water, electricity and telephone services. On the one hand, we have to privatize, but when we attempt to put our policy of renewable energy into action, the multinationals frustrate every effort we make, as they are only interested in the rate of return."

The Johannesburg Summit seemed oblivious to the fact that increasing poverty throughout the world, shown especially in the food and water crises, can only intensify conditions of desperation that lead to terrorism and other violence. This missed opportunity was a serious blow to sustainable development and demonstrated once again the power of vested interests.

Climate Warming and Health Warning

Correcting the imbalance between military spending and efforts to reduce poverty would create a better quality of life for people on a worldwide scale and foster a more harmonious global community. This is an ethical issue of enormous proportions. I will return later in this book to the ethics of human security issues. I end this discussion of the effects of militarism on a fragile planet with two more examples of the degradation and human suffering caused by society's misplacement of priorities. One of these examples is the state of the planet itself; the other is a galloping plague affecting the world's most vulnerable.

Climate change affects everyone, scientists say, as they gain greater understanding of the link between emissions of greenhouse gases, climbing global temperatures, rising sea levels, and intensity of extreme weather events. The Worldwatch Institute says current atmospheric carbon dioxide is at its highest level in 420,000 years. The 1990s were the warmest decade since precise measurements began in the nineteenth century, and a 10- to 20-centimetre rise in average global sea levels was recorded in the 1990s. Small island nations, representing 5 per cent of the world's population, face not only economic ruin but physical extinction from rising seas in a world that is rapidly heating up. The Intergovernmental Panel on Climate Change, a group of more than 250,000 scientists from around the world, says "most of the warming of the past 50 years is attributable to human activities."

The hard fact is the collapse of the earth's environment has already begun. The Aleutian Islands ecosystem has collapsed, the world's coral reefs are rapidly dying, one in four mammal species will be threatened with extinction in the near future, glacial and ice sheets worldwide are melting as global temperatures rise, and fish populations are decreasing. Again, human activity is responsible for much of this. Despite the evidence of the effects of greenhouse gases, the global emission of carbon increased 9 per cent in the past decade, with much of the increase attributed to the industrialized, developed world. US emissions alone rose 18 per cent between 1990 and 2000. Nonetheless, the US abandoned its commitment to the Kyoto Protocol, a key diplomatic initiative to control carbon emission, whose origins stem from the Rio Summit. The Kyoto accord would merely bring emissions back to 1990 levels, but even this modest target has been fought by corporate interests focused more on the state of company finances than the state of the planet.

This lack of compassion is also evident in the international response to the scourge of HIV/AIDS, a disease that was practically unknown just a generation ago. Today, dozens of countries are in the grip of serious HIV/AIDS epidemics and many more are on the brink. Nearly 25 million people have died of AIDS since the first clinical evidence was reported in 1981; in 2001, 5 million became infected, 800,000 of them children. According to UNAIDS, the UN agency dedicated to the disease, between 65 and 100 million people will die of AIDS by 2020. Sub-Saharan Africa is by far the worst-affected region in the world. Although 28.5 million people there have the disease, fewer than 300,000 have received antiretroviral drugs. Africa's HIV/ AIDS catastrophe is a humanitarian disaster of historic proportions. In parts of the continent, the adult infection rate exceeds 30 per cent, and in some places more than 40 per cent of pregnant women are infected. Populations are being decimated and children orphaned.

No single factor, biological or behavioural, determines the spread of the HIV/AIDS infection. Most HIV/AIDS transmission occurs through unprotected sexual intercourse, with unsafe blood transfusions and injections accounting for a small fraction. The rejection of condoms by sexually active men exacerbates the transmission rate. A high number of sexual partners has consistently been found to be associated with greater likelihood of infection, but the chances of individuals engaging with commercial sex workers—and thus having more partners—is clearly enhanced in societies with large numbers of single, migrant men. These communities, such as those found in the mining belts of southern Africa, are the result of a complex interplay of economics and history. Forced relocation due to war, long-term travel along transit routes for commercial classes, and the lack of livelihoods are all factors. In Africa, young women have consistently been found to have a higher rate of HIV infection than men of the same age group. Social and cultural conditions, which limit women's control over their own sexuality, play a role in the spread of the disease, particularly among young people.

Though hardest hit, Africa is not alone in this misery. In Eastern Europe and Central Asia, the assumption that the epidemic would remain confined to marginalized groups, such as intravenous drug users, is turning out to be wishful thinking. The explosive growth of HIV/AIDS is wreaking havoc on the populations it inflicts. Experts say the epidemic is spreading to Russia, India, and China, and is bringing immense economic consequences with it.

Prevention programs and antiretroviral drugs may slow the spread of the epidemic, but so far governments have been tight-fisted. At the UNAIDS world conference in 2002, Kofi Annan called for $7 billion to $10 billion a year to fight AIDS, but donor countries pledged only $2 billion. Later, in his 2003 State of the Union address, President Bush pledged $15 billion over five years to fight global AIDS. *The New York Times* commented: "As Mr. Bush prepared for possible war with Iraq, his new commitment to global AIDS suggests an emerging geopolitical reality: If the United States is going to present itself as having a moral imperative to stop terrorism, it must also take up the cause of morality in a manner that does not involve dropping bombs." Bush's action did not look so magnanimous when it was later revealed the money for AIDS would be taken from programs to combat child poverty. Stephen Lewis, the former Canadian diplomat who is the Secretary-General's Special Envoy for HIV/AIDS in Africa, warned that we cannot allow HIV/AIDS to become "collateral damage" in the Iraq war. "Wars have their own dynamic," he said, "in the wake of which hopes can be strangled and dreams can be suffocated."

If the communicable scourge of AIDS grows unchecked, its multiple effects could cascade across society, further heightening the risk of insecurity. Recognizing the security implications of AIDS, the UN Security Council in 2000 adopted a resolution that highlighted the potential threat the epidemic poses for international security, particularly in conflict and peacekeeping settings. It is, of course, on human security (that is to say, on people's right to safety from the threats to personal security) that AIDS has its most devastating effects. Many of the world's most marginalized countries, especially those where HIV/AIDS is causing its worst damage, need long-term international co-operation and financial support. But since 1990, Official Development Assistance provided to the 28 countries with the highest HIV/AIDS rate has fallen by a third. In that same period, world military expenditures totalled approximately $10 trillion.

The misguided priorities of governments, which rush to feed the culture of war while skimping on programs to build human security in a suffering and fragile world, are outrageous and tragic.

3

The Massive Lie of Nuclear Weapons

The culture of war is built upon the enormous lie that weapons bring security. Nowhere is this lie more pronounced than in the rationale for the maintenance of nuclear weapons. It is a fundamental argument of this book that any use of nuclear weapons today would constitute a criminal act—a crime against humanity.

The very idea of a nuclear weapon is to kill massively. UN studies have shown that the social and economic consequences of nuclear war in a world intimately interconnected in life-support systems would be catastrophic. Patterns of economic production, distribution, and consumption would be completely disrupted. The severe physical damage from blast, fire, and radiation in the target countries would preclude the type of support that made recovery possible following World War II. The prospect of widespread starvation as a consequence of nuclear war would confront both target and non-target nations. The human impact would be made even worse by a breakdown in health-care facilities and transportation services. Such descriptions of the overwhelming effects of nuclear weapons are not found in the general political and military literature on the subject. This immense threat is covered, instead, by a veil of generalities, platitudes, and obfuscation.

A group of international experts known as the Canberra Commission on the Elimination of Nuclear Weapons said in 1996:

> The proposition that nuclear weapons can be retained in perpetuity and never used—accidentally or by decision —defies credibility. The only complete defence is the elimination of nuclear weapons and assurance that they will never be produced again.

An enforceable regime to shut down the production of all nuclear weapons and fissile materials and oversee the dismantling of all nuclear weapons is essential.

Reflecting on the total number of nuclear weapons still in existence is staggering. The estimated number is 34,145. This number is an improvement over the 65,000 nuclear weapons in existence during the mid-1980s. But is the world supposed to be satisfied that the current number allows the world to be blown apart only, say, 100 times rather than 200? The destructive power of the world's nuclear arsenal is beyond comprehension. Reduced numbers will not make the world safe, but rather the complete elimination of these weapons. Far from grappling with their responsibility before it is too late, the major powers are running away from it.

It is a counter-productive political policy for the five permanent members of the UN Security Council to think that they can have the exclusive right to possess nuclear weapons while other countries are prohibited from acquiring them. The responsibility for the looming prospect of a nuclear war of some dimension can be laid squarely on the US, Russia, the UK, France, and China. They have been warned time and again that their refusal to honour their legal obligation to negotiate the total elimination of their nuclear arsenals is leading to the breakdown of the Non-Proliferation Treaty (NPT).

The NPT, which came into force in 1970, was designed to stop the proliferation of nuclear weapons. The total of 188 countries party to the NPT makes it the largest arms

Country	Strategic Warheads	Tactical Warheads	Warheads in Storage	TOTAL
United States	7,013	1,620	5,000	13,633
Russia	5,858	4,000	9,421	19,279
TOTAL				32,912
Per cent of Total				96 per cent

United Kingdom	200
France	350
China	400
India	35
Pakistan	48
Israel	200
TOTAL	**34,145★**

*Data for the US and Russian arsenals is taken from the Carnegie Endowment for International Peace (see www.ceip.org/files/pdf/Policybrief23.pdf) and, for the other nuclear weapons states, the Natural Resources Defense Council (see www.nrdc.org/nuclear/nudb/datainx.asp). It should be noted that estimates of the composition and evolution of the arsenals for China, Israel, India, and Pakistan are extremely difficult to make and these figures are necessarily estimates. The Stockholm International Peace Research Institute calculates the total number of nuclear warheads at 36,800.

control and disarmament treaty in the world. Only three countries that possess nuclear weapons—India, Pakistan, and Israel—remain outside the treaty. North Korea and Iraq and perhaps a few other states have tried to build them. South Africa relinquished its small nuclear arsenal, and Brazil and Argentina ended their nuclear weapons programs.

When the NPT was indefinitely extended in 1995, the nuclear powers made three promises:

1) A comprehensive Nuclear Test Ban Treaty would be achieved by 1996.

2) Negotiations on a convention to ban the production of fissile material for nuclear weapons would come to an "early conclusion."

3) "Systematic and progressive efforts globally" to eliminate nuclear weapons would be made, and all states would make similar efforts for general and complete disarmament under strict and effective international control.

Five years later, at the NPT 2000 review, the NPT took another step forward through securing from the nuclear weapons states "an unequivocal undertaking to accomplish the total elimination of their nuclear arsenals." This commitment was embodied in a program of 13 Practical Steps, to which all parties to the NPT agreed in guiding their systematic and progressive efforts to implement Article VI of the NPT. This calls for states to "pursue negotiations in good faith" for nuclear disarmament.

How have the pledges of 1995 stood up? The Comprehensive Test Ban Treaty (CTBT) was actually negotiated and opened for signature in 1996. It obliges all parties not to conduct "any nuclear weapons test explosion" in any environment. A Partial Test Ban Treaty had been achieved in 1963, which shut off atmospheric testing but allowed underground tests. Since 1963, 1,450 tests had taken place.

For the CTBT to enter into force, 44 states must ratify it; these 44 are named because they all possess nuclear reactors. Former President Bill Clinton of the US was the first to sign the CTBT, but the US Senate rejected ratification in 1999 in a vote that was construed as being as much anti-Clinton as anti-CTBT. When George W. Bush assumed the presidency in 2001, the US turned its back on the CTBT and walked away from the treaty altogether. Since the US has withdrawn its support of the CTBT, entry-into-force is now effectively blocked.

India, Pakistan, and Israel—members of the list of 44—are also delinquent. India says that since nuclear weapons are the currency of power, as evidenced by the five permanent members of the Security Council, it must have them. Pakistan will not let itself be overtaken by its arch-rival, India. Israel has quietly built its nuclear stocks based on the claim that only the possession of nuclear weapons can save it from being overrun by the Arab world. One can be forgiven for thinking that nuclear disarmament goes in circles.

The CTBT, the first promise made by the nuclear powers in 1995, was at least negotiated. The second pledge, to bring to an "early conclusion" negotiations on a convention to ban the production of fissile material—such as enriched uranium and plutonium—for nuclear weapons, ran into a brick wall at the Conference on Disarmament (CD) in Geneva. The CD is the permanent body for disarmament maintained by its 66 members, who report to the UN. The conference operates by consensus, but it cannot even agree on a format for negotiations, let alone carry them out. Countries such as India and Pakistan want existing stocks of fissile material maintained by the nuclear weapons states to be taken into account; the major states want the negotiations to focus on blocking new stocks. China resists any negotiations unless they are linked to negotiations to prevent an arms race in outer space. It argues that if the US persists in the weaponization of space, then China may have to rebuild its nuclear stocks. The US adamantly refuses any meaningful discussions on keeping space free from weapons. In fact, the missile defence system now being built is paving the way for space-based weapons, which will give the US military control of space.

The third pledge, "systematic and progressive efforts globally," to eliminate nuclear weapons, has been subjected to the subterfuge that has characterized the nuclear disarmament agenda for more than three decades. The Moscow Treaty, signed May 24, 2002, by President Vladimir Putin of Russia and President Bush, provides the latest example. The treaty was applauded because it would reduce the number of deployed strategic warheads on each side to a range of 1,700 to 2,200 by 2012; this is down from the current 6,000 to 10,000. But an examination of the fine print shows that the treaty does not provide for these weapons to be actually dismantled and thus does not meet the key principle of irreversibility, one of the 13 Practical Steps agreed to in 2000. Neither does it include any verification procedures, another step that was agreed upon. Not only are the delivery systems not destroyed, but large numbers of nuclear weapons can be held as a "responsive force" and as "spares."

Thus the announced reduction of strategic warheads to 1,700 to 2,200 turns out to allow the arsenals of both countries to maintain several times more nuclear weapons (both tactical and strategic, deployed and reserves) for the indefinite future. This is sleight-of-hand nuclear disarmament. When we add the fact that both the US and Russia (even though the Cold War has ended) keep close to 5,000 nuclear weapons on hair-trigger alert, able to be fired on 15 minutes notice, it is obvious that they treat nuclear disarmament as a game. The International Court of Justice has ruled that states have an obligation not only to pursue negotiations for nuclear disarmament, as required by the NPT, but to conclude such negotiations. The UK, France, and China refuse to enter comprehensive negotiations until the US and Russia reduce their stocks to the level of hundreds rather than thousands.

The pledges that the principal nuclear weapons states have made are hollow and worthless. Bruce Blair is president of the Washington-based Center for Defense Information. In writing recently of his meetings with groups of American government officials and military officers, he said, "Not a single person of the many hundreds I have polled voiced the belief that the true intention of the United States is, or ever has been, to abolish nuclear weapons." In fact, Blair added, "some consider the question itself to be almost frivolous because the prospect of nuclear abolition is deemed so remote as to be implausible." The other nuclear states are just as devious.

The failure to implement the NPT, now a third of a century old, portends a dark future. Why should non-nuclear weapons states believe the promise of the NPT? The pledges made in 1995 have been abandoned. The ruling of the International Court of Justice has been ignored. The "unequivocal undertaking" toward total elimination, given in 2000, has been pushed aside. Jayantha Dhanapala, former UN Under-Secretary-General for Disarmament Affairs, calls the gulf between declaration and actual deeds "alarming." Instead of genuine progress in nuclear disarmament, the world has seen the abrogation of the Anti-Ballistic Missile (ABM) Treaty, the development of improved nuclear weapons, the prospect of more nuclear tests, and plans for the use of nuclear weapons even against non-nuclear weapons states. Each day, the warning of the Canberra Commission rings more true: "The possession of nuclear weapons by any state is a constant stimulus to others to acquire them."

The danger of such terrible weapons being used is growing. This was indicated when the Doomsday Clock, maintained by the Chicago-based *Bulletin of the Atomic Scientists,* moved forward to just seven minutes to midnight. This is the closest it has been to midnight since the 1980s— the height of the nuclear arms race between the US and the Soviet Union. Today, India and Pakistan are trigger points. While the Soviet-American relationship was based on the mutual interest of deterrence with nuclear security systems in place, India and Pakistan are locked in a territorial dispute over Kashmir. Pakistan's regime is shaky. As neighbours, India and Pakistan would have scant seconds to distinguish between a nuclear accident and a threat. North Korea also poses a danger to the world. Its threats to rescind its membership in the NPT and engage in missile testing have destabilized Asia. While the possession of a nuclear weapon by any state must be deplored, it cannot be over-emphasized that the nuclear weapons states hold the major responsibility for setting up legal regimes to ensure the elimination of all nuclear weapons.

The US and the Future of Nuclear Weapons

While none of the other nuclear weapons states can be exonerated from their responsibilities to the world community, the United States is in the dominant position of deciding which way the world will go on nuclear weapons: toward permanence or toward elimination. The US is not only the Western leader, the linchpin of NATO, and the strongest military power in the world, it has now become the colossus on the world stage. There is no one who can challenge its goal of "full spectrum dominance" in air, on land, on the sea, and in space. It is futile to speak of nuclear disarmament without focusing intensely on the role of the US.

In the aftermath of the terrorist attacks of September 11, 2001, the US entered a new period in its history. Throughout the Cold War, it relied on the strategies of containment and nuclear deterrence to hold its adversary, the Soviet Union, in check. Under the strategy of nuclear deterrence, nuclear weapons are meant only to deter a potential aggressor from attack, knowing that the recipient has sufficient nuclear capability to retaliate massively. But with the advent of suicidal extremists, striking even from within its borders, the US has adopted a policy aimed at preventing attacks before they occur. This has led to stringent internal security measures affecting the entry into the country by foreign-born nationals, and has produced a startling new doctrine of pre-emptive attack, first used against Iraq in 2003.

President Bush's National Security Strategy, announced on September 20, 2002, says the US will take anticipatory action to defend itself, even if uncertainty remains as to the time and place of the enemy's attack. The strategy states: "To forestall or prevent ... hostile acts by our adversaries, the United States will, if necessary, act preemptively." This doctrine is intended to prevent potential foes, whether states or terrorist groups, from even threatening to use weapons of mass destruction. The Bush doctrine seeks to adapt the traditional concept of imminent threat to modern conditions where terrorists can strike suddenly. International law does not countenance pre-emptive attacks in self-defence unless there is compelling evidence of an imminent attack. The idea of any state claiming the unilateral right to pre-emptive attack on another turns existing international law upside down, and it does a complete end run around the Charter of the UN.

The new National Security Strategy must be seen in the context of the Nuclear Posture Review (NPR). During 2001, the Bush Administration conducted an NPR, which showed that its nuclear weapons stockpile remains a cornerstone of US national security policy. The NPR, though initially a report by the Department of Defense, has the status of a policy document. It underpins the Moscow

Treaty of 2002 and was cited as the principal justification for the 2003 National Nuclear Security Administration budget request to Congress. The NPR establishes expansive plans to revitalize US nuclear forces and all the elements that support them, within a new triad of capabilities that combine nuclear and conventional offensive strikes with missile defences and nuclear-weapons infrastructure. The NPR assumes that nuclear weapons will be part of US military forces for at least the next 50 years; it plans an extensive and expensive series of programs to modernize the existing force, including a new intercontinental ballistic missile to be operational in 2020 and a new heavy bomber in 2040. The NPR says that there are four reasons to possess nuclear weapons: to "assure allies and friends," "dissuade competitors," "deter aggressors," and "defeat enemies."

It also lists specific scenarios for using nuclear weapons: A conflict with China over Taiwan, a North Korean attack on South Korea, and an attack by Iraq on Israel or another neighbour. The new policy means that the US will threaten the use of nuclear weapons against countries that do not themselves possess nuclear weapons; such an action runs counter to the NPT. Thus, under the guise of participating in nuclear disarmament through the dismantling of excess nuclear weapons, the US is actually widening the role of nuclear weapons far beyond the deterrence measures against the former Soviet Union in the Cold War. US intentions are stated clearly in the NPR:

> Nuclear weapons play a critical role in the defence capabilities of the United States, its allies and friends. They provide credible military options to deter a wide range of threats, including WMD [weapons of mass destruction] and large-scale conventional military force. These nuclear capabilities possess unique proportions that give the United States options to hold at risk classes of targets [that are] important to achieve strategic and political objectives.

The Review notes that the Department of Energy's National Nuclear Security Administration will undertake several new initiatives, including:

- Possibly modifying existing weapons to provide additional yield flexibility in the stockpile.

- Improving earth-penetrating weapons to counter the increased use by potential adversaries of hardened and deeply buried facilities.

- Designing warheads to reduce "collateral damage."

Resuming nuclear testing is contemplated. New personnel will be trained in nuclear skills, nuclear test diagnostic capabilities modernized, and additional field experiments conducted. Although the primary intention is to use conventional arms in pre-emptive raids on suspected nuclear, biological, and chemical weapons facilities, US officials have spoken of the utility of using nuclear weapons. For this purpose, the US is conducting research for a new low-yield nuclear weapon. This "bunker-buster" could be used with earth-penetrating missiles to destroy underground command and control bunkers and hidden facilities used for developing or storing weapons of mass destruction. The bunker-buster bomb, at first developed in laboratories, well-financed by the Stockpile Stewardship Program, may well be headed for explosive testing.

The proponents of this first-strike weapon claim it will be "low-yield," meaning that it will have an impact only on its immediate surroundings. Actually, a radioactive cloud seeping from the crater would release a plume of radioactive gases that would irradiate anyone in its path. If it were used to root out terrorists near a major city, such as Baghdad, the casualties could be in the hundreds of thousands. Nonetheless, Pentagon officials feel the development of a "mini-nuke"—about one-quarter the size of the atomic bomb dropped on Nagasaki and less than one-hundredth that of most of the weapons in the existing US arsenal—could gain public support. A mini-nuke, which would be more usable, would be seen as a "credible threat" to prevent nations and terrorists from developing underground hideouts. Advocates hope to replace the public's general fear of nuclear attacks with the notion that a US first strike may be necessary in today's geopolitical environment.

Russian President Vladimir Putin has been quick to respond to the Bush Administration's new nuclear strategy with his own plans to develop low-yield nuclear weapons. In his 2003 annual address to the Duma, Putin said: "I can inform you that at present the work to create new types of Russian weapons, weapons of the new generation, including those regarded by specialists as strategic weapons, is in the practical implementation stage." No sooner had these words been uttered than the US Congress voted to end the ban on research and development of low-yield nuclear weapons, thus moving the development of the new age of nuclear weapons out of the laboratories into active preparation. It is astounding that, in the light of this development, the US representative at the 2003 Geneva meeting of the parties to the Non-Proliferation Treaty declared: "We are not developing new nuclear weapons. The United States has no current requirement for a new nuclear warhead. The United States has not lowered the threshold for nuclear weapons use. ..." The fact is the US, with Russia struggling to keep up, has led the way into the new generation of nuclear weapons. This will only encourage other countries, such as North Korea and Iran, to build their own nuclear weapons as fast as possible.

Concerned about a widened rationale for the use of nuclear weapons, ten US senators, led by Senator Edward M. Kennedy of Massachusetts, sent a letter on February 21, 2003, to President Bush, expressing "grave concern" about US policy. Kennedy rejected any policy that contemplated the use of nuclear weapons against a non-nuclear state.

...Such a shift in U.S. policy would deepen the danger of nuclear proliferation by effectively telling non-nuclear states that nuclear weapons are necessary to deter a potential U.S. attack, and by sending a green light to the world's nuclear states that it is permissible to use them. Is this the lesson we want to send to North Korea, India, Pakistan, or any other nuclear power?

Present US activities can hardly be said to be in the spirit of the "unequivocal undertaking" which was promised in 2000. They are not faithful to the "good faith" requirements of Article VI. The US takes umbrage at the suggestion that it is not acting in good faith and points to its dismantling of more than 13,000 nuclear weapons since 1988. The Administration notes with pride that it has paid for the removal of nuclear weapons from Ukraine, Belarus, and Kazakhstan. It further claims that, through the Moscow Treaty, it is moving forward to the overall goal of nuclear disarmament. Yet at the first meeting of the Preparatory Committee for the 2005 Non-Proliferation Treaty Review, held in 2002, the US openly and unashamedly admitted that it "no longer supports" two of the 13 NPT Practical Steps: the ABM Treaty and the CTBT. Despite its previous commitments, the US spokesperson said the US claims the right to set its own rules with respect to the NPR. The government stated:

> The new U.S. approach will consist of nuclear and non-nuclear offensive systems, active and passive defense, and a revitalized defense infrastructure. These elements are interrelated, but have one thread in common—a reduced reliance on nuclear weapons.

From this statement, the US went on to vote "no" to a resolution at the UN Disarmament Committee which was intended to uphold the 13 Practical Steps. The resolution was introduced by the New Agenda Coalition, a group of seven states—including Brazil, Egypt, Ireland, Mexico, New

Zealand, South Africa, and Sweden—which is leading the way at the UN for the preservation of the NPT. The US was joined in rejecting the resolution by its NATO nuclear partners—the UK and France—and the effect of this action dragged all but one of the non-nuclear NATO partners down to an abstention. Only Canada voted in favour. Two years earlier, all of NATO (with only France abstaining) had voted in favour of a resolution of similar intent. This was considered great progress at the time, since NATO's Strategic Concept holds that nuclear weapons are "essential."

In 1999, Canada persuaded NATO to review the Strategic Concept, but nothing came of this effort, since the US adamantly opposed the exercise. At least 180 tactical nuclear weapons are stationed on the soil of six European NATO countries, which are ostensibly non-nuclear: Belgium, Greece, the Netherlands, Germany, Italy, and Turkey. The UK and France, as nuclear powers, have their own arsenals. All NATO countries are caught in an incoherent posture of holding to the NATO doctrine that nuclear weapons are necessary, on the one hand, while, on the other, wearing their NPT hats and pledging an "unequivocal undertaking" to get rid of them. They are virtually silent on the wreckage of the arms control and disarmament agreements carefully built up over the past three decades. While the US and its nuclear weapons partners are valiantly challenged by the New Agenda Coalition, the Nuclear Weapons States (NWS) cannot easily be dissuaded, since they hold the power of veto in the Security Council.

With the NPR naming Iran, Iraq, Libya, Syria, and North Korea as possible targets of US nuclear weapons, another of the hallmarks of the NPT is being violated. At the time of the 1995 NPT extension, the nuclear powers pledged not to use nuclear weapons against non-nuclear parties to the NPT. This pledge was called a negative security assurance, and, while the Nuclear Weapons States gave non-nuclear states their word, they refused to make it legally enforceable.

New US nuclear policies foreseeing a war-fighting role for nuclear weapons and open advocacy of pre-emptive attack have weakened the rule of law, on which the UN was founded, and have severely crippled the NPT. Without a clear-cut US commitment to the NPT, the treaty is unlikely to survive.

Meanwhile, the US is proceeding to develop a missile defence system that will stimulate a renewed nuclear arms race. China is not alone in rejecting a situation in which the US has an impenetrable shield (if it even works) as well as a policy of pre-emptive attack. Space weapons are on the horizon, since the missile defence system will evolve into a mix of ground and space sensors and weapons. The US Space Command has presented its twenty-first-century vision of military dominance in space to protect US interests and investments. The Command states that existing land, sea, and air missions will be enhanced by space systems. While the Outer Space Treaty, which prohibits placing nuclear weapons in space, has not been directly challenged, the intention to weaponize space with a military system that integrates nuclear and non-nuclear offensive systems will kill the basis of trust on which the NPT stands.

Although no country can at present rival or contest US space dominance, it would be a mistake to underestimate the rapidity with which other states are beginning to use space-based systems to enhance their security. The weaponization of space should be blocked by an early treaty, but there is little prospect of this. Science is making space warfare possible, and scientific discoveries advancing the technology of warfare have always been used.

Similarly, a new development called nanotechnology, still in its early stages, may revolutionize warfare yet again by constructing artificial atomic and molecular structures capable of destroying environments and life forms from within. This evolving field of atomic and molecular engineering has been hailed as a breakthrough in improving health and other quality-of-life indicators. But the dark side of nanotechnology has been recognized by strategists who see it as a possibility for achieving a new level of effectiveness in fighting wars.

For the past several years, Secretary-General Annan has tried to get the major powers to agree to a special international conference to identify nuclear dangers, but the nuclear states will not even agree to this, let alone take the required actions. The majority of countries want to hold a Fourth Special Session on Disarmament to move the world agenda forward, following the three previous special sessions in 1978, 1982, and 1988. Again, the proposal is stonewalled. Undoubtedly, the major states recall all too well the stirring language and Action Programme of the Final Document of the 1978 session, which has been called "the bible" of nuclear disarmament.

> Removing the threat of a world war—a nuclear war—is the most acute and urgent task of the present day. Mankind is confronted with a choice: we must halt the arms race and proceed to disarmament or face annihilation.

The Action Programme in 1978 called for urgent, comprehensive negotiations for the complete elimination of nuclear weapons with "agreed time-frames" for implementation. The US joined in the consensus achieved by this document. But 1978 was in the Administration of Jimmy Carter. Shortly afterward Carter lost power to Ronald Reagan, who in his eight years in the presidency doubled US spending on defence and initiated 49 new weapons systems. On the eve of receiving the 2002 Nobel Peace Prize, Carter criticized his own government's failure to lead the way to obtain enforceable agreements to ban all weapons of mass destruction. "Quite often the big countries that are responsible for the peace of the world set a very poor example for those who might hunger for the esteem or the power or the threats that they can develop from nuclear weapons themselves," he said.

In 1988, ten years after the First Special Session, Prime Minister Rajiv Gandhi came to the UN with a plan for the elimination of nuclear weapons by 2010. "Our plan calls upon the international community to negotiate a binding commitment to general and complete disarmament. This commitment must be total. It must be without reservation." The nuclear powers rejected the proposal. Eleven months later, India successfully tested the Agni, its new intermediate-range ballistic missile capable of delivering a nuclear warhead up to 2,500 kilometres. Gandhi was assassinated in 1991. Also in 1988, Mikhail Gorbachev brought to the UN a 15-year-plan for the elimination of nuclear weapons in three stages. He received a standing ovation from delegates in the General Assembly. Within two years, the Soviet Union collapsed and Gorbachev lost power.

A Terrorist Catastrophe

Faced with a constantly modernizing US nuclear arsenal and new high-tech systems of which missile defences are only one part, existing nuclear weapons states are likely to retain their nuclear stocks. And more states, seeing that nuclear weapons are the true currency of power, may follow India, Pakistan, and Israel and acquire nuclear weapons. The danger of a nuclear catastrophe grows.

That catastrophe may well be set off by terrorists. Immediately after September 11, UN Secretary-General Kofi Annan went to Ground Zero in New York and said that, as horrible as the destruction was, it would have been much worse had the terrorists used nuclear devices. He called on nations to "re-double" efforts to fully implement the relevant treaties to stop the spread of nuclear and other weapons of mass destruction. In the case of the NPT, it is not a multiplication of efforts we are witnessing, but a subtraction.

The lack of an enforceable convention to shut off the development and production of nuclear weapons and fissile materials has resulted in the new risk of nuclear terrorism. There has been resolution after resolution at the UN for a Nuclear Weapons Convention; the resolutions actually pass with handsome majorities. Public opinion polls throughout the world show that people favour abolishing all nuclear weapons. But the major states will have none of it. They categorically refuse to enter such negotiations, so determined are they to preserve their nuclear strength. Now the world faces not only the prospect of a nuclear war between states but the use of a nuclear weapon by terrorists who have stolen nuclear materials. Russia has experienced 18 thefts of fissile materials, and so worried is the US that it pays to safeguard the Russian system. The systems in India and Pakistan are not even inspected by the International Atomic Energy Agency (IAEA), which has the international responsibility of ensuring that safeguards are in place. The annual budget of the IAEA is scarcely more than the $100 million the US spends every day to maintain its nuclear arsenal. The IAEA is so starved for funds that it depends on voluntary contributions to fund its new anti-terrorism program, which costs $12 million per year.

In this new era of suicidal terrorism, the threat of attacks using weapons of mass destruction has grown exponentially. Virtually all experts on the subject say it is not a question of whether a massive attack will occur, but when. A great hole could be blown in the heart of any city by a black-market nuclear warhead produced from an existing arsenal, or by an explosive homemade device using stolen components. A toxic fog of radiation would spread many kilometres from the epicentre, leaving a path of death and sickness in its wake. A one-kiloton explosion (one-fifteenth the power of the bomb detonated over Hiroshima) in Times Square would kill 20,000 people in a matter of seconds. The lethal fallout from a mushroom cloud of irradiated debris would blossom more than 160 kilometres (100 miles) in the air, and then drift back to earth, showering people deep in the New York boroughs and New Jersey. Such an event would have consequences that, while hard to predict in the form of retaliation, would so destabilize international relations that the law of the jungle might well replace the rule of law.

Biological and Chemical Weapons

Although obstacles can be overcome, it is very difficult to obtain the materials and produce an explosive nuclear device. It is much easier to obtain the radioactive material for a non-nuclear "dirty bomb," such as cobalt-60—readily available in hospitals for use in radiation therapy—dissolve it and introduce it into the ventilation systems of office buildings or subways. According to the International Atomic Energy Agency, the radioactive materials needed to build a dirty bomb can be found in almost any country in the world, and more than 100 countries may have inadequate control and monitoring programs necessary to prevent or even detect the theft of these materials. Such a radiological attack would cause, in addition to countless deaths, panic in the population.

A hint of the threat posed by other weapons of mass destruction occurred following the September 11 events when anthrax spores mailed through the US postal system infected 23 persons, killing five. A fine powder, anthrax is contracted by inhalation or skin contact of infected spores of the bacterium. Anthrax is a preferred agent for biological weapons development owing to its ease of acquisition and cultivation as well as to its lethality and hardy nature. A biological weapon can be made cheaply in a small building, even in the back of a truck, and easily transported. The threat of bioterrorism derives from easy access to biological agents and technology as well as from the blurred border between peaceful and offensive uses of biotechnology.

While biological warfare has long been considered repugnant to the conscience of humanity, biological weapons have been developed and used for almost 3,000 years. We may have come a long way from heaving animal carcasses into enemy fortifications, but the general idea of spreading disease through bacterial toxins has been preserved. The past century saw considerable advances in the development and delivery of biological toxins—such as botulinum, ricin, anthrax, and yersinia pestis. Today, along with nuclear bombs, weapons of mass destruction can be in the form of a bacteriological agent that can cause great numbers of deaths through its ability to spread in the person, animal, or plant attacked. Though the world took pride in eradicating smallpox, one of the most devastating diseases known to humanity, concerns persist about clandestine stocks of the virus being used as weapons by states or terrorists.

Despite signing the Geneva Protocol in 1925 banning offensive use of bio-weapons, a number of European countries developed them during the 1930s and 1940s. Japan used biological weapons in its attack on China during World War II. In 1975, the Biological and Toxins Weapons Convention came into force, obliging the 145 states parties not to develop or produce biological toxins. This was the first global treaty abolishing a class of weapons of mass destruction, but it had no mechanisms for monitoring or verifying compliance. Seeking to redress this omission, states began to negotiate a legally binding Protocol to the Treaty in 1995. Suddenly, in 2001, the US rejected the draft text, because it would violate the commercial confidentiality demanded by pharmaceutical manufacturers and open "biodefence" facilities to scrutiny. The Review Conference of 2001 broke down, and it took a year of diplomatic work to produce an agreement to at least keep measures to control the use of biological weapons on the negotiating table.

Like its biological partner in death, chemical warfare dates to antiquity. During the Peloponnesian War (431–404

B.C.), the Spartans used arsenic smoke. During the siege of Constantinople (637 A.D.), the Byzantine Greeks employed "Greek Fire"—a mixture of petroleum, pitch sulphur, and resins. The first modern use of chemical weapons occurred during World War I, when the German army released hundreds of tons of chlorine gas at Ypres, killing and wounding thousands of Allied troops. Commonly, chemical weapons, delivered as a gas or a liquid, choke victims by causing a build-up of fluid in the lungs, which then causes asphyxiation. Once inside the body, only a minute particle is required to inhibit the body's neural activity, leading to vomiting, convulsions, paralysis, and near-certain death. By the end of the war, more than 100,000 deaths were directly attributed to poison gas. Egypt used chemical weapons in North Yemen (1963–67). Iraq used them heavily against Iran during the Iraq-Iran War (1983–88), while Iran also used them against Iraq. On March 20, 1995, members of the Aum Shinrikyo religious cult launched a terrorist attack with sarin nerve gas in a Tokyo subway system, killing 12 people and injuring 5,000. Several states—Iraq, Libya, North Korea, and Syria—are suspected of maintaining stocks of chemical weapons, despite a ban on their production.

The world has long struggled to rid itself of chemical weapons; the first attempts go back to 1675, when a Franco-German accord that restrained both armies from using poisoned bullets was signed. The horrors of World War I drove the creation of the Geneva Protocol in 1925, which banned the use (but not the development) of chemical and bacteriological weapons. In 1961, the American and Soviet governments pledged to consider the disarmament of chemical weapons in tandem with their nuclear and biological arsenals. The talks broke down in the Cold War atmosphere, and it took until 1997 before a Chemical Weapons Convention entered into force. The treaty bans the production and development of chemical weapons. It includes a stringent verification system providing for "routine" inspections of chemical industry facilities and "challenge" inspections, which can be conducted at any location provided three-quarters of the governing body do not block the challenge. The costs to destroy chemical weapons can be prohibitive, and some states, such as Russia, have sought economic assistance.

It is a strange logic that the nuclear powers have supported (with varying degrees of warmth) global conventions banning the production of biological and chemical weapons, but continue to adamantly oppose a similar convention banning the production of nuclear weapons. All three—biological, chemical, and nuclear—are weapons of mass destruction. Perhaps, upon examination, it is not so strange. Biological and chemical weapons have long been considered the "poor man's" weapon. They can be produced relatively cheaply and the ingredients are not hard to obtain. But nuclear weapons are an elite form of destruction. High technology has been necessary and, until recently, this expertise and the ability to manufacture nuclear weapons components have been available only to the powerful nations. The nuclear weapons states and veto-wielding members of the Security Council have been able to exercise a hegemony over the rest of the world with their military strength. They have always claimed that nuclear weapons are necessary for their security. This is not true. But even if it were true, why would not non-nuclear states claim the right to the same weapons for their security?

Nuclear weapons are not about security; they are about power, and they are the most vivid expression of the culture of war. With more countries wanting into the nuclear club, they are gradually losing their elitism. In fact, since biological and chemical weapons are officially banned, nuclear is becoming the poor man's weapon of choice. Racism also enters this quagmire. India objected to Western denial of nuclear status to India, claiming that the West felt that the brown and black people of the world could not be trusted with nuclear weapons, whereas whites could. As the white population diminishes in the twenty-first century, the idea that the rest of the world—non-white—will acquiesce to Western nuclear domination is both fanciful and dangerous. Only because China, too, has nuclear weapons has the racism charge so far been muted. But racism and economic strength are interwoven in the determination of the powerful to maintain their nuclear weapons.

"The Ultimate Evil"

The culture of war has a very strong hold on public thinking. In fact, while people aspire to peace and say they support abolition of all weapons of mass destruction, they uncritically continue to accept the lies produced by the propaganda apparatuses of governments that nuclear weapons are essential to their security. There is in the public mind what the psychologist Robert Jay Lifton has called "a collective form of psychic numbing" about nuclear weapons. Misleading official statements and government secrecy have contributed to a societal amnesia. When the subject does surface, there is a form of denial about the lessons of Hiroshima and Nagasaki. When the Smithsonian Institution planned an exhibit at the National Air and Space Museum in Washington, D.C., to mark the 50th anniversary of Hiroshima and Nagasaki in 1995, political pressure from Congress resulted in the removal of any artifact or photo depicting the actual bomb-damage. Rather than coming to terms with the bombing, and what it should mean in the modern context, Americans continue to treat Hiroshima and Nagasaki as a threat to their national self-image.

The nuclear powers would not be able to so blithely carry on with their nuclear weapons program if world consciousness, raised out of the war culture to a new recognition of this evil, demanded abolition. But world consciousness has been dulled. We have lived with the bomb so long that it has insinuated itself into our thinking. Hiroshima and Nagasaki seem so long ago, and are but a blur in memory. The abolition movement seeks to open the eyes of society to what the former President of the International Court of Justice called "the ultimate evil." Society is certainly not impervious to evil: the Holocaust, slavery, and genocide have all been recognized as the evils they truly are. But the ultimate evil appears to be too far removed from daily life to engage our attention. It is almost as if the issue is too big to handle.

The moral case against nuclear weapons is clear-cut. Nuclear weapons not only assault life on the planet, they assault the planet itself, and in so doing they assault the process of the continuing development of the planet. This is an affront to the Creator of the universe, an affront to the mysterious process of God's creation that makes a connection between us and an unfathomably distant past that the present generation has no right to interrupt. Nuclear weapons lure us into thinking we can control the destiny of the world. They invert order into disorder. Nuclear weapons are evil because they destroy the process of life itself. Nuclear weapons are supposed to be governed by the covenants of humanitarian law. In fact, a full-scale nuclear war would destroy the very basis of humanitarian law. The structure of our civilization would disappear. Nuclear weapons, with no limitation or proportionality in their effect, make a mockery of old just war theories. How can self-defence be cited as a justification for the use of nuclear weapons when their full effect destroys the "self" that is supposed to be defended?

During the Cold War, political acceptance of nuclear weapons to deter "the enemy" became the overriding consideration. When the Soviets disappeared from the political scene as the enemy, the nuclear establishment had to find a new one. This time the enemy is some political leader or terrorist, now or in the future, who will threaten the West with a nuclear weapon. The circle of fear, perpetuated by those with a vested interest in maintaining nuclear weapons, is unending. Unchallenged, this is a trap from which humanity will never escape.

Nuclear proponents must now be challenged, for, in clinging to spurious, self-serving rationales, they are deliberately deceiving the world. Humanity faces the gravest of futures if the world is to be ruled by militarism and the culture of war rather than law. The doctrine of nuclear deterrence can no longer claim the slightest shred of moral acceptance: it is morally bankrupt. The dangers of proliferation make it essential to tell policy-makers that nuclear weapons are immoral. Military doctrines justifying the maintenance of nuclear deterrence must be forthrightly condemned. Nuclear planners would then be deprived of any further claim to moral legitimacy.

Similarly, in the legal realm, the time has come for governments to formally declare that the use of nuclear weapons is unlawful based upon the rules of international humanitarian law. A world ruled by law is the only hope for a peace with security and stability. The International Court of Justice has made a profound contribution to de-legalizing nuclear weapons by reaffirming the cardinal principles of humanitarian law:

> In order to protect the civilian population, states must never use weapons that are incapable of distinguishing between civilian and military targets.

> It is prohibited to cause unnecessary suffering to combatants, and hence states do not have unlimited freedom of choice of weapons.

The Court ruled that the threat or use of nuclear weapons would contravene all aspects of humanitarian law and called for negotiations toward total elimination to be concluded. The so-called loophole in the Court's Opinion—that the Court could not decide whether the use of nuclear weapons would be legal in cases of extreme self-defence—must now be closed. It is a canard to state, as nuclear proponents do, that a nuclear weapon can be used in a proportionate or limited way, even using "low-yield" weapons in defence.

Nuclear weapons cannot, of course, be abolished in a vacuum. An architecture for security must be built: verification procedures, mechanisms to combat cheating, and an enforceable rule of law. The nuclear proponents say they cannot divest as long as there are regional conflicts that hold back the development of an architecture that can guarantee security without nuclear weapons. This argument, too, must be turned on its head. The determined maintenance of nuclear weapons by the powerful few is the factor that inhibits the processes of building the conditions for peace in regions of conflict.

The Mayor of Hiroshima, Tadatoshi Akiba, exposed, once again, the massive lie of nuclear weapons when he spoke to the 2003 meeting of the NPT parties:

> ... Those who stand to lose wealth, prestige and control in a peaceful world are determined to maintain high levels of fear and hatred. Gullible publics are being persuaded that only a powerful military backed by nuclear weapons can protect them from their enemies.

The Mayor of Hiroshima warned that we stand today on the brink of "the actual use of nuclear weapons." That terrifying prediction ought to galvanize the public to demand a total ban on nuclear weapons, and it ought to energize governments to negotiate and implement a Nuclear Weapons Convention. The very idea that a small group of wealthy and powerful individuals should have the power over government policies that spend billions of dollars on military overkill while so many people live in life-threatening poverty is intolerable.

This corrupt power continues to drive world systems and it will only be broken when enough people stand up to demand that this Armageddon be removed from our heads. Fortunately, there are signs that increasing numbers of people are trying to push forward new ideas to counteract the twisted logic of nuclear weapons. This work is starting to build a culture of peace to replace the scourge of the culture of war. It is to this work, providing a solid basis for a new hope for humanity, that I now turn.

PART II

The Culture of Peace

4

Life in Full Vibrancy

On March 12, 1930, Mohandas Gandhi, known in history as the Mahatma, or Great Soul, launched his seminal move in a life dedicated to showing that non-violence could overcome violence. With 78 followers, he set out on a march to the coast of India to make salt from the waves by a traditional Indian method. One way the British had kept Indians poor and dependent was by taxing salt, a basic and important commodity, especially in Indian cooking. Britain insisted that it earn money from the manufacture and sale of all salt. Gandhi believed this to be yet another unjust law, so he flagrantly and publicly violated it as a symbol of his objection to British rule. By the time he reached the sea, people from all across the land had joined in the march. Gandhi and his followers were arrested; soon more than 60,000 Indians filled the jails. It would take many more acts of non-violent resistance, but eventually the Viceroy began negotiating with Gandhi, and India achieved independence in 1947.

Although the present government of India has shunned Gandhi's principles of non-violence, his lesson has lived on and influences many people around the world today. Born in 1869 in the Indian region of Porbandar, Gandhi came from a wealthy background. He travelled to London to get a law degree and later moved to South Africa, where he worked as a lawyer for Indian merchants. He was already a member of the *Swadeshi* movement, which threatened the British economic hold on India by urging South Asians to avoid buying products and goods made by the British and exported to India. Military rebellion against the British had not worked, and it seemed to Gandhi that the British kept on wringing more wealth from their colony at every turn. In South Africa, he came face to face with more suffering and poverty of underprivileged peoples. White South Africans imposed harsh taxes on Indians to make sure they did not become politically powerful.

Gandhi's opposition to this discrimination led him to develop his ideology of non-violent resistance. He called his approach *satyagraha*, which in Sanskrit means insistence on truth. He believed that the injustices such as those practised by white South Africans were so blatantly wrong that, simply by living and working according to one's own principles, one could change and ultimately overcome one's oppressors without ever resorting to violence. By putting this philosophy into practice, Gandhi and his followers managed to soften some of South Africa's racist laws.

Returning to India in 1915, he immediately started helping those who were most oppressed and poverty-stricken. In 1919, when British soldiers killed 400 unarmed Indians who had gathered in a plaza in Amritsar to protest Britain's enactment of "emergency" powers, Gandhi began staging non-violent protests and violating unjust British laws. In his hunger strikes, undertaken to stop the violence between Hindus and Muslims, he came close to death, but these hunger strikes were admired throughout the world. Dismayed by the continued violence between Hindus and Muslims, Gandhi refused to celebrate when Britain granted independence. Though his example of non-violence had stopped the rioting, Gandhi was himself assassinated by a Hindu fanatic on January 30, 1948.

Martin Luther King, Jr., achieved similar world acclaim for his advocacy of non-violence as a strategy for social change. A strong believer that violence in the struggle for racial justice is both impractical and immoral, King won the Nobel Peace Prize in 1964. Born in Atlanta in 1929, King's roots were in the African-American Baptist Church. He greatly admired black social gospel proponents, such as his father, who saw the church as an instrument for improving the lives of African-Americans. When the policy of segregation was at its height, he became a pastor and accepted the pastorate of Dexter Avenue Baptist Church in Montgomery, Alabama.

In 1955, five days after Montgomery civil rights activist Rosa Parks refused to obey the city's rules mandating segregation on buses, black residents launched a bus boycott and elected King president of the Montgomery Improvement Association. As the boycott continued during 1956, King gained national prominence through his exceptional oratorical skills and personal courage. His house was bombed and he was convicted along with other boycott leaders on charges of conspiring to interfere with the bus company's operations. Despite these attempts to suppress the movement, Montgomery buses were eventually desegregated after the US Supreme Court declared Alabama's segregation laws unconstitutional.

King went on to found the Southern Christian Leadership Conference, emphasizing the goal of black voting rights. He toured India to increase his understanding of Gandhian non-violent strategies. The black protest movement spread. King was often in conflict with younger militants, who were not at all convinced of the merits of non-violence. Although Malcolm X's message of self-defence and black nationalism—expressing the anger of northern, urban blacks—challenged King's moderation, he never wavered. In 1963, King and his staff guided mass demonstrations in Birmingham, Alabama, where local white police officers—known for their anti-black attitudes—used police dogs and fire hoses on protesters. King used to say that "Bull" O'Connor, the Commissioner of Public Safety, was happy when a black threw rocks, but he was unhappy when the protesters remained non-violent. "He knows how to deal with violence, but he does not know how to handle non-violence." President John F. Kennedy reacted to the Birmingham protests by agreeing to submit civil rights legislation to Congress (which passed in 1964 under Lyndon Johnson). Mass demonstrations in many communities culminated in a march on August 28, 1963, that attracted more than 250,000 protesters to Washington, D.C. Addressing the marchers from the steps of the Lincoln Memorial, King delivered his famous "I Have a Dream" oration. He was assassinated on April 4, 1968, after assisting a garbage workers' strike in Memphis. After his death, King remained a controversial symbol of the African-American civil rights struggle, revered by many for his martyrdom on behalf of non-violence and condemned by others for his insurgency.

In one of his sermons, dealing with Jesus' admonition to love your enemies and do good to those who hate you, King rejected the idea that Jesus was an impractical idealist. "Far from being the pious injunction of a utopian dreamer, this command is an absolute necessity for the survival of our civilization." He added: "There is a power in love that our world has not discovered yet. ... Mahatma Gandhi discovered it ... but most men and women never discover it. For they believe in hitting; they believe in an eye for an eye and a tooth for a tooth; they believe in hating for hating; but Jesus comes to us and says, 'This isn't the way.'"

Like Gandhi, King believed that non-violence means more than simply refraining from violence. It is also a way of taking positive action to resist oppression or bring about change. The appeal of non-violence is that it directly challenges the logic (or illogic) of trying to make the world a more peaceful place by using violence as a tool. Gandhi and King's non-violence involved often spectacular techniques: peaceful demonstrations, sit-ins, picketing, vigils, fasting and hunger strikes, work stoppages, blockages, and other forms of civil disobedience. Though civil disobedience was one tool, their core principles did not rely on this technique. They promoted the kind of peaceful activity that is easy to take up—after a belief in non-violence takes hold.

The ideas of Gandhi and King not only live on, they flourish in an organization called A Season for Non-Violence, a group based in the US and made up of prominent peace activists. Each year it convenes 64 days (January–April) of educational, media, and grassroots events in many cities that create an awareness of non-violent principles and practices as powerful ways to heal, transform, and empower people. Local groups hold symposia on interfaith and inter-racial healing, workshops, Days of Dialogue, Prayer and Meditation, children's theatre, essay contests, artistic and cultural events, and memorial marches. Members of peace organizations and members of religious, business, arts, and education institutions join. At the fifth anniversary celebrations of A Season for Non-Violence in 2002 at the UN, Arun Gandhi, the Mahatma's grandson, and Yolanda King, King's daughter, led off a round of speeches praising the Gandhi-King principles for non-violent social change.

Since the world is still a violent place, it is hard to measure the full effect of what Gandhi and King started. More time is needed for the seeds of non-violence to be cultivated and to grow in the culture of war, which has dominated human activity for 5,000 years. Other heroic figures have, in their own ways, moved the agenda for non-violent social change forward.

One figure is Nelson Mandela, who, despite 27 years' imprisonment by the apartheid regime of South Africa, has never answered racism with racism and has become a force for reconciliation between blacks and whites. After his release in 1990, Mandela said, "My message to those of you involved in this battle of brother against brother is this: take your guns, your knives, and your *pangas* [machetes], and throw them into the sea. Close down the death factories. End this war now!" His countryman, Archbishop Desmond Tutu, ebullient and spirited, became the leading spokesman for non-violent resistance in the 1980s. "I am near tears," he once said. "If the only thing that we ever did was to say strongly to people, please stop the violence, we will have advanced the kingdom of God in an incredible way."

Immediately after September 11, 2001, the Dalai Lama appealed for a non-violent response to the terrorism as a much more productive long-term strategy. "It will be seen as hypocrisy to condemn and combat those who have risen in anger and despair, but to continue to ignore those who have consistently espoused restraint and dialogue as a constructive alternative to violence," he said.

Mother Teresa, whose canonization is proceeding rapidly, cared for the homeless, dying outcasts of India and, in so doing, awoke the consciences of millions. "Love one another," she said. "Bring that peace, that joy, that strength of presence of each other, and we will be able to overcome all the evil that is in the world."

In 1980, Archbishop Oscar Romero of El Salvador spoke out against terror, torture, and murder by the military and demanded a peace that can only be found in human rights and assurances of basic dignities. "In the name of God, in the name of this suffering people whose cry rises to heaven more loudly each day, I implore you, I beg you, I order you: stop the repression." The next day, he was shot and killed at his altar while offering Mass.

While these advocates of non-violence and social change became famous, myriad people around the world, in their daily lives, espouse the same ideas. Of course, their work appears overwhelmed by the advanced technology of destruction. So overpowering is the culture of war that it discourages many from even thinking that they could be instruments of change. A deep cynicism and mistrust are deeply imbedded in populaces. Many who do speak up for change are dismissed as idealists. Yet, despite a political and societal climate that supports the entrenched culture of war status quo, there are significant signs that a culture of peace is being born. Already the ideas and formulation of a culture of peace have taken shape and been given a structural basis. A culture of peace may still be a goal rather than the dominant reality, but, just as Gandhi and King's principles of non-violence were taken up by many, so, too, the programs for a culture of peace are slowly taking shape.

A New Vision of Peace

The idea of a culture of peace to overcome—in a non-violent way—the culture of war was first taken up at a conference of scholars in 1989 at Yamoussoukro, Ivory Coast. It was conceived as a "new vision of peace" constructed "by developing a peace culture based on the universal values of life, liberty, justice, solidarity, tolerance, human rights and equality between men and women." The conference endorsed the Seville Statement of 1986 (see Chapter 1), which showed that violence is not an endemic part of the human condition. The essential ideas of a culture of peace were then developed into a memorandum by David Adams, a professor of psychology at Wesleyan University in Connecticut, who was spending 1992 as a sabbatical year at the UN Educational, Scientific and Cultural Organization (UNESCO) in Paris.

The purpose of UNESCO is to contribute to peace and security by promoting collaboration among the nations through education, science, and culture. The goal is to further universal respect for justice, for the rule of law, and for human rights and fundamental freedoms that are affirmed for the peoples of the world, without distinction of race, sex, language, or religion. The Constitution of UNESCO says that just as war begins in the minds of individuals, so must peace. Thus the organization seeks to "build the defences of peace" in the minds of individuals.

Adams presented his memo to Federico Mayor, UNESCO's Secretary-General. The timing was fortuitous. The Cold War was over; the Gulf War of 1991 showed the need for a stronger peace apparatus; UN peacekeeping operations were proceeding in Cambodia, Mozambique, and Angola; and UNESCO had initiated a peace project in El Salvador as a contribution to the peace accords of that country. Adams, who had come to UNESCO as a specialist on the brain mechanisms of aggressive behaviour, the evolution of war, and the psychology of peace activists, was invited by Mayor to join the organization. For the next decade he guided the Culture of Peace project through the shoals of bureaucracy. He eventually became the Director of the Unit for the International Year for the Culture of Peace.

UNESCO began to formulate a culture of peace as a set of ethical and aesthetic values, habits and customs, attitudes toward others, forms of behaviour, and ways of life that draw on and express:

- Respect for life and the dignity and human rights of individuals

- Rejection of violence

- Recognition of equal rights for men and women

- Support for the principles of democracy, freedom, justice, solidarity, tolerance, the acceptance of differences, and

- Communication and understanding between nations and countries and between ethnic, religious, cultural, and social groups.

A culture of peace is an approach to life that seeks to transform the cultural tendencies toward war and violence into a culture where dialogue, respect, and fairness govern social relations. In this way, violence can be prevented through a more tolerant common global ethic. The culture of peace uses education as an essential tool in fostering attitudes supportive of non-violence, co-operation, and social justice. It promotes sustainable development for all, free human rights, and equality between men and women. It requires genuine democracy and the free flow of information. It leads to disarmament.

Adams set out the contrasting alternatives between a culture of war and a culture of peace:

CULTURE OF WAR	CULTURE OF PEACE
enemy images	understanding, tolerance, and solidarity
armaments and armies	disarmament, general and complete
authoritarian governance	democratic participation
secrecy and propaganda	free flow of information and knowledge
violence (structural and physical)	respect for all human rights
male domination	equality between women and men
education for war	education for a culture of peace
exploitation of the weak and of the environment	sustainable economic and social development

The culture of peace is, at its core, an ethical approach to life. It recognizes that the world is experiencing a fundamental crisis. Though this crisis is often expressed in economic, ecological, or political terms, it is fundamentally a crisis of the human spirit. It is a crisis of all humanity that, in the journey through time, has reached the point where we are capable of destroying all life on earth just at the moment when the recognition of the inherent human rights of everyone is beginning to take hold. It illuminates our choice in how to live and which path we will follow. The culture of peace offers the vision of a global ethic toward life in full vibrancy; the culture of war offers the prospect of misery and annihilation.

An early example of a culture of peace in action is seen in the success of UNESCO's Culture of Peace pilot project in El Salvador. In 1992, the UN mediated an end to a bloody 12-year civil war that had claimed 80,000 lives and uprooted one million people. With the help of UNESCO, conflict was transformed into co-operation by involving those groups previously caught up in violence in the planning and implementation of human development projects of benefit to all. One such project involved the production of daily radio broadcasts and educational campaigns directed at the most needy in the country. Although the conflicting groups were distrustful of each other at first, UNESCO successfully brought them together; they have since learned to negotiate and engage in concerted decision-making. A rigorous UNESCO evaluation of the El Salvador project confirmed the value of the Culture of Peace program.

This successful model holds important lessons that UNESCO has tried to apply to Mozambique, Burundi, and the Philippines. But despite the proven success in El Salvador, UNESCO has been unable to get the needed support and funding from developmental agencies, which, for various reasons, are not interested. Considering the resources available, the culture of peace could be extended beyond any one country's situation and embrace the development of a global culture of peace movement.

In 1995, UNESCO's General Conference decided that the Culture of Peace would be its priority program. The goal was to ensure the transition from a culture of war, violence, imposition, and discrimination toward a culture of non-violence, dialogue, tolerance, and solidarity. Mayor implemented the decision in three main ways. First, he undertook an intensive personal diplomacy with heads of state and the leaders of international organizations. Second, he established a special project ,"Towards a Culture of Peace," to engage UNESCO sectors in a series of co-ordinated activities. Third, he proposed an additional human right, the human "right to peace" (which I will discuss in Chapter 5). In this personal commitment to a human right to peace, Mayor showed himself to be an unusual official indeed.

Born in 1934 in Barcelona, Spain, Mayor had an early childhood marked by civil war, and his adolescence and adulthood were lived in the shadow of hot and cold war on the European continent. He became a scientist, dedicating his research to ensuring the proper development of the brain in infancy. As an educator, he stood for academic freedom and the social responsibility of the university. He became convinced that violence is never inevitable and that the culture of war need not be a permanent fixture. He was the right man to promote UNESCO's core ethical mission of tolerance and dialogue.

Mayor wrote a book responding to the end of the Cold War, *The New Page: Culture of War and Culture of Peace*. Here he stated that permanent mobilization for conflict could and should give way to a new spread of democracy that, fostering the development process, would help greatly to reduce the causes of war. He scorned the industrialization of war into a monstrous mass enterprise in which war becomes a socially organized activity for introducing sharp pieces of steel into the bodies of young men. The extremism of the 1920s and 1930s exalted the state and led to the bombing of civilian populations. More technological refinements for killing followed. This led Mayor to ponder how to get rid of the baggage of the past, which we carry into each new technological development. "In a culture of war," he said, "all bodies, all mentalities, all souls, if you will, are permanently tensed for the worst. The 'other' in another camp, another country, another continent, is a threat. Differences between individuals and communities become rallying points for mobilization and hatred, not simply the rich pluralism history has given us."

Science, technology, art, and communication then become weapons or buttresses to secure us from our enemies, and soothe us in the righteousness or superiority of our cause or identity. Government is expected to protect us with ever more destructive and sophisticated weapons systems. We are told that we can sleep well each night because soldiers, sailors, and airmen are awake and ready to launch missiles and ensure that "they"—the others—will never launch theirs. The weapons become so secret that the civilian leadership of nations may not be trusted to understand their own arsenal. Perhaps the worst aspect of the culture of war, Mayor felt, is our constant definition of "us" against "them," in which we divide the world into hostile groupings.

> We have attached so many labels onto others—and they onto us—that we may have lost sight of that most basic, enormous truth: the other is a woman, a child, a man, capable of love, uniquely capable of receiving and giving love, uniquely valid and valuable and human. Dare we reach out and take the risk that every major religion and philosophy says we must, the risk of loving and being loved?

In the midst of this age-old culture of war, there have been visionaries or rebels who could not or would not conform. Individuals, men and women, have understood that war is not necessarily a solution to the problems confronting society. They have not only abhorred war morally but also understood historically that war has rarely provided a definitive or stable solution to problems between or within nations. Indeed, Mayor said, every culture and every great religion has a strand in it emphasizing that which is common and peaceful between us and that forms the basis for dialogue instead of hostility and aggression.

This thinking has challenged the waste of young lives, the sacking of great cities, and the loss of great cultural memories. By the end of World War II, artists and writers, academics, and politicians were ready to explore a multilateral vision of a potential culture of peace. The UN was born and with it a family of agencies and world programs dedicated to meeting human needs. For its part, UNESCO, through its supporters around the world—teachers, scientists, writers, journalists, and artists—sought to advance, in the broadest way, a culture of peace through education, culture, science, and communication. Now, Mayor said, there is an urgency to this work to head off a "shared catastrophe" caused by the explosive chemistry of environmental degradation and dehumanizing poverty.

As UNESCO Secretary-General, Mayor dedicated himself to directing the organization's energy into three initiatives to develop a culture of peace:

1) A proposal for an International Year for the Culture of Peace (2000)

2) A proposal for a UN Declaration and Programme of Action on a Culture of Peace

3) An initiative of the Nobel Peace Laureates' "Campaign for the Children of the World" that would eventually become the International Decade for a Culture of Peace and Non-Violence for the Children of the World (2001–10).

The centrepiece of this work is the Declaration and Programme of Action on a Culture of Peace adopted by the UN General Assembly on September 13, 1999. It is perhaps the most comprehensive program for peace ever taken up by the UN. Its chief promoter, Ambassador Anwarul Chowdhury of Bangladesh, who later became the UN's High Representative for Least Developed Countries, Landlocked Developing Countries and Small Island Developing States, hailed it for bringing together all the elements for peace in a way the Assembly had rarely touched in its 50-year history.

The Declaration should be examined closely to see its scope. Article 1 sets out the framework for a culture of peace.

A culture of peace is a set of values, attitudes, traditions, and modes of behaviour and ways of life based on:

- Respect for life, ending of violence, and promotion and practice of non-violence through education, dialogue, and co-operation

- Full respect for the principles of sovereignty, territorial integrity, and political independence of States; and non-intervention in matters that are essentially within the domestic jurisdiction of any State, in accordance with the Charter of the UN and international law

- Full respect for and promotion of all human rights and fundamental freedoms

- Commitment to peaceful settlement of conflicts

- Efforts to meet the developmental and environmental needs of present and future generations

- Respect for and promotion of the right to development

- Respect for and promotion of equal rights and opportunities for women and men

- Respect for and promotion of the right of everyone to freedom of expression, opinion, and information

- Adherence to the principles of freedom, justice, democracy, tolerance, solidarity, co-operation, pluralism, cultural diversity, dialogue, and understanding at all levels of society and among nations.

The fuller development of a culture of peace is integrally linked to:

- Promoting peaceful settlement of conflicts, mutual respect and understanding, and international co-operation

- Complying with international obligations under the Charter of the UN and international law

- Promoting democracy and development, and universal respect for and observance of all human rights and fundamental freedoms

- Enabling people at all levels to develop skills of dialogue, negotiation, consensus-building, and peaceful resolution of differences

- Strengthening democratic institutions and ensuring full participation in the development process

- Eradicating poverty and illiteracy, and reducing inequalities within and among nations

- Promoting sustainable economic and social development

- Eliminating all forms of discrimination against women through their empowerment and equal representation at all levels of decision-making

- Ensuring respect for and promotion and protection of the rights of children

- Ensuring free flow in information at all levels and enhancing access thereto

- Increasing transparency and accountability in governance

- Eliminating all forms of racism, racial discrimination, xeno-phobia, and related intolerance

- Advancing understanding, tolerance, and solidarity among all civilizations, peoples, and cultures, including toward ethnic, religious, and linguistic minorities

- Realizing fully the right of all peoples—including those living under colonial or other forms of alien domination or foreign occupation—to self-determination enshrined in the Charter of the UN.

The Programme of Action on a Culture of Peace includes eight areas of action:

- Education

- Sustainable economic and social development

- Respect for all human rights

- Equality between women and men

- Democratic participation

- Understanding, tolerance, and solidarity

- Participatory communication and the free flow of information and knowledge

- International peace and security.

Implementing such an extensive Programme of Action is a long-term challenge, and this is why the UN called for partnerships to develop toward "a global movement for a culture of peace" among various actors (governments, civil society, and the UN system). The Programme would be aimed not only at the 2000 International Year for the Culture of Peace, but also at the decade that followed. In preparation for the year, Nobel Peace Prize Laureates drafted Manifesto 2000, translated into more than 50 languages, to act as a guideline for practical actions and public awareness campaigns:

- *Respect all life*: Respect the life and dignity of each human being without discrimination or prejudice.

- *Reject violence*: Practice active non-violence, rejecting violence in all its forms: physical, sexual, psychological, economical, and social, in particular towards the most deprived and vulnerable, such as children and adolescents.

- *Share with others*: Share my time and material resources in a spirit of generosity to put an end to exclusion, injustice, and political and economic oppression.

- *Listen to understand*: Defend freedom of expression and cultural diversity, giving preference always to dialogue and listening without engaging in fanaticism, defamation, and the rejection of others.

• *Preserve the planet*: Promote consumer behaviour that is responsible and development practices that respect all forms of life and preserve the balance of nature on the planet.

• *Rediscover solidarity*: Contribute to the development of my community, with the full participation of women and respect for democratic principles, in order to create together new forms of solidarity.

The high point of the media campaign was the simultaneous launch of the International Year in more than 100 countries. In support of the manifesto, the signatures of more than 74 million individuals in every region of the world were presented to the President of the UN General Assembly. These signatures included 37 million in India; 15 million in Brazil; 11 million in Colombia; and more than one million in Japan, Kenya, Nepal, and the Republic of Korea. The NGO-UNESCO Liaison Committee promoted partnership agreements with 180 international organizations, which carried out wide-ranging projects, including entertainment, workshops, sporting events, festivals, and Internet sites to promote the Year. Schools joined in, and teacher-training programs were developed.

Case studies of women's peacebuilding experiences were undertaken in several African states, and a regional conference, "Asian Women for a Culture of Peace," was organized in Vietnam. In Guatemala, 5,000 graduating students were given special training in peace themes. In Mali, weapons were burned in a ceremony to symbolize the end of the armed struggle that had previously torn that country apart. Civil society groups in many cities in Russia carried out projects that led to the creation of a Federal Programme on Tolerance and Prevention of Extremism in Russian society. In Bosnia and Herzegovina, 1,000 young people of diverse origins became involved in an exercise to learn more about each other and their respective cultures to promote ethnic tolerance. The Young Peacemakers Club, begun in the US to promote positive skills to build peace, has spread around the world. The list of projects continues into the areas of human rights, poverty, gender, democratic participation, sustainable development, and information technology. Many individuals and groups have been inspired to help advance these issues.

This surge of activity culminated in the General Assembly resolution that 2001–2010 would be designated the International Decade for a Culture of Peace and Non-Violence for the Children of the World. Each year of the International Decade has a different focus, with the UN Year of Dialogue Among Civilizations providing the first theme. Annan said the purpose is "to bring nations, cultures and civilizations ever closer together through dialogue and cooperation" and is a "central pillar" of the global response to conflict. The theme, which seeks to promote the best of humanity, took on even greater significance in the wake of September 11, which represented the worst of humanity.

Several countries, including Austria, Canada, Germany, Poland, and Japan, launched events to bring people of different backgrounds together to understand one another's viewpoints better. One of the most important contributions was made by UNESCO, which organized a dialogue that was incorporated into a book, *Crossing the Divide: Dialogue Among Civilizations*. I will discuss this in Chapter 7.

A Social Movement is Building

It seems strange that the UN resolution delineating the culture of peace does not contrast its elements with the culture of war to make the point that revolutionary changes in thinking are required. Strange, that is, until one remembers that the Western governments have always been reluctant to pursue programs explicitly designed to build peace and absolutely hostile to any action that would infringe on their right to make war. A government cannot start a war if its people do not believe in the power of force and if they are not convinced there is an enemy. These same governments have made sure that UNESCO's funding was kept at a low level, so that, good local programs notwithstanding, it has never been able to become a powerful international force. "The powerful member states hesitate to empower an agency that might call into question the very basis of their power and wealth, the culture of war," says David Adams. When Mayor left UNESCO in 1999, the Culture of Peace program lost its most ardent spokesman. UNESCO's work is now on a decidedly lower key, but the Organization's Web site reveals it is continuing wide-ranging projects throughout the world. (See the annotated list of Web sites at the end of the book for this and other sites related to the Culture of Peace.)

UNESCO's current Secretary-General, Koichiro Matsuura, says: "A global movement in the finest sense is emerging: a marshalling of all existing forces for social improvement arising from the world's civil societies and a mobilization of their energies, ideas and commitments."

Since UNESCO remains the lead agency for promoting the activities throughout the UN system for the International Decade, the ardour with which it pursues its mission will play an important role in implementing the content of the Culture of Peace resolution. But UNESCO, in getting the project off the ground, has already played perhaps its most important role. Since a culture of peace is essentially about values, its implementation will depend very much on how the forces of religion, education, and civil society will advance the concept.

The culture of peace cannot survive only as a program of an international agency. Its meaning extends beyond the wording of UN resolutions. Creating and nurturing a culture of peace is a social movement. It requires a profound transformation in our thinking and acting. No wonder governments are perplexed by it, for the culture of peace challenges the status quo. It is a counter-cultural way of life to the culture of war. It will not be achieved overnight or in a decade, but the International Decade can help us maintain focus on the many dimensions of peacemaking.

The culture of peace should not be considered the technical solution to every world problem; rather, it supplies the moral foundation for establishing a better individual and global order—a vision that can lead individuals away from despair and society away from chaos. Though religion does not have an ownership of the formulation of moral standards, religions are especially well placed to advance the standards of a culture of peace. There already exists among religions a consensus for the values, standards, and moral attitudes that are the basis for a global ethic. Despite their own various failures, the world's religions bear a responsibility to promote the binding values, convictions, and norms that are valid for all humans regardless of their nationality, social origin, skin colour, or religion.

Along with religious formation, general education has a fundamental role in advancing a culture of peace. The UN, somewhat reticent to discuss religious values for fear of stumbling into old controversies surrounding the linkage of religion to the state, has felt freer to state clearly that education at all levels is one of the principal means to build a culture of peace. The resolution says that children, from an early age, benefit from education on the values, attitudes, modes of behaviour, and ways of life to enable them to resolve any dispute peacefully in a spirit of respect for human dignity, tolerance, and non-discrimination. Educational curricula should be revised and teacher training undertaken in conflict prevention. New initiatives in peace education can be implemented by institutions of higher learning.

The UN resolution revealed the dynamic of the social revolution required by stating:

> A key role in the promotion of a culture of peace belongs to parents, teachers, politicians, journalists, religious bodies and groups, intellectuals, those engaged in scientific,

philosophical and creative and artistic activities, health and humanitarian workers, social workers, managers at various levels as well as to non-governmental organizations.

It is evident that many of the above groups of people are intimately involved in projects that fall within the culture of peace. However, seeing the cultures of war and peace as a constantly evolving dynamic tension helps to develop a momentum for change. The movements of ecology, human rights, women's equality, democracy, and nuclear disarmament—though each is distinctive in its own right—need each other for full effect. Recognition of the interdependence of its various components is one of the most important contributions that an increasingly influential civil society can make to the culture of peace.

These three components—religion, education, and civil society—are all so vital to the implementation of the culture of peace that I devote a chapter to each in the third part of this book.

Finally, in elaborating a culture of peace, it is necessary to deal with the inertia, opposition, and cynicism that remain such powerful obstacles to its implementation.

Since September 11, a deep sense of fear has pervaded the general populace. We have been violently attacked. We have been told that we do not know where the next attack is coming from. We must be ready. We must prepare ourselves for this new kind of aggression. If pre-emptive attacks are necessary, so be it. We must fight a war against this unseen enemy. Media relentlessly feed us images of destruction and ceaselessly convey the message that the military's might is now necessary to protect us. The culture of war was given a great gift by the terrorists of September 11. If you want peace, the Romans said, prepare for war. The terrorists have apparently confirmed this statement.

In this environment, the culture of peace can hardly be heard, let alone obtain the political attention and government funding to make an impression on electorates. In addition to being fearful, many are cynical about peace ever being achieved in such a turbulent world. The arms manufacturers, who mount such powerful lobbies in the legislative halls of Western countries, discount the elements of peace as so much naïveté. Worse, to challenge militarist thinking is to run the risk of being considered unpatriotic. The fences enclosing creative thinking are indeed high.

In the past, the machinery of war has not built the kind of world in which people everywhere can achieve human security. Why can it be expected to do so today? Rather, it is the slow, painstaking construction of a new culture of peace that offers hope for a better future. The values of such a culture are well worth the time developing them takes. The momentum of history, buttressed by new life-enhancing technologies, is on the side of the culture of peace.

5

Peace: A "Sacred Right"

The work already accomplished in the UN system to develop the concept of the human right to peace is one of the world's best-kept secrets. The culture of war so pervades public opinion that it has drowned out voices asserting that the human right to peace is a fundamental right of every human being and is, in fact, the major precondition for all human rights. The time has come to emphasize that the peoples of the world have a sacred right to peace.

That very concept—"the peoples of our planet have a sacred right to peace"—was inserted into the first operative paragraph in the Declaration on the Right of Peoples to Peace, adopted by the UN General Assembly on November 12, 1984. One does not need to be reminded of the countless deaths in wars that have occurred in the almost two decades following. Such a recounting does not invalidate the UN Declaration, it only underlines the point that this right needs to be better understood before procedures are developed to enforce it under the rule of law.

The intimate linkage between human rights and peace was first recognized in the Preamble and in Articles 1 and 55 of the UN Charter; in Article 28 of the Universal Declaration of Human Rights; and in the Covenant on Civil and Political Rights, and the Covenant on Economic,

Cultural, and Social Rights. The Preamble to the Charter, in stirring language evoked by the ashes of World War II, affirms that the peoples of the UN are determined "to practice tolerance and live together in peace with one another as good neighbours." Article 1 proclaims as the first purpose of the UN the maintenance of international peace and security. Written a few years later, the Preamble to the Universal Declaration of Human Rights states, "The recognition of the inherent dignity and the equal and inalienable rights of all members of the human family is the foundation of freedom, justice and peace in the world." These documents affirm the right of states to peace through a "peace system" with the primary goal being the preservation of peace and a respect for human rights as essential to the development of friendly relations among nations.

Taken together, these documents provide a basis for the human right to peace, but it was not until 1978, when the UN General Assembly adopted the Declaration on the Preparation of Societies for Life in Peace, that the right to peace began to take shape in a more formal way. The Declaration states:

> ...every human being, regardless of race, conscience, language or sex, has the inherent right to life in peace. Respect for that right, as well as for the other human rights, is in the common interest of all mankind and an indispensable condition of advancement of all nations, large and small, in all fields.

In setting out ways to implement this principle, the Declaration calls upon countries to ensure that their international and national policies are directed toward achieving life in peace, especially with regard to younger generations. This emphasis on national duty and youth would become the central elements in later elaborations of the right to peace.

The Declaration was given a boost with the 1981 African Charter on Human and Peoples' Rights, which proclaimed that all peoples have the right to national and international peace and security. Article 3 declared firmly: "Human beings are inviolable. Every human being shall be entitled to respect for his life and the integrity of his person. No one may be arbitrarily deprived of this right."

Like its 1978 counterpart adopted by the General Assembly, the African Charter places the onus for ensuring the right to peace on governments, but also emphasizes the individual citizen's duty to work toward the right to peace.

Subsequently, the UN General Assembly adopted the Declaration on the Right of Peoples to Peace in 1984. After affirming the principle that "the peoples of our planet have a sacred right to peace," the resolution declares that the preservation of the right of peoples to peace "constitute[s] a fundamental obligation of each State." The Declaration went on to state that the exercise of this right demands "the elimination of the threat of war," particularly nuclear war. (It was undoubtedly this reference to the elimination of the threat of nuclear war that caused multiple abstentions by Western states. Although the vote was 92 in favour and none opposed, there were 34 abstentions and the Declaration could not be implemented.) Although the Declaration does not explicitly declare the right to peace as a "human" right, it can be argued that its intent was just that. This is clear in the assertion that:

> …life without war serves as the primary international prerequisite for the material well-being, development and progress of countries, and for the full implementation of the rights and fundamental human freedoms proclaimed by the United Nations…

In this statement, the right to peace is considered the fundamental prerequisite for the fulfillment of other basic rights. For instance, the Declaration understands that economic development is only possible in the presence of peace. It links human rights, development, and peace as three conditions that cannot exist in isolation from one another. Simply stated, without peace every other right is illusory. Thus—and in retrospect—even in 1984 the UN was responding to a changing international environment with the kind of innovative thinking needed to lift up humanity to confront the challenges of globalization.

A Major Diplomatic Effort

Only with the end of the Cold War in the 1990s did work toward the right to peace grow from a few sentences in international agreements into a major diplomatic effort. This new push was, in part, a product of the hopeful climate surrounding the end of the superpower rivalry. However, the 1997 Declaration of a Human Right to Peace by UNESCO's Director-General, Federico Mayor, was very much a response to the many conflicts that had consumed one society after another earlier in the decade. (See the Appendix for the full text of this important document.) The wars in Iraq, Somalia, Yugoslavia, Rwanda, and elsewhere left a sense that the international community had taken a wrong turn after the end of the Cold War and was missing a golden opportunity to build a better foundation for peace. This window of opportunity was the driving force behind the UNESCO Director-General's call to get back on track and build the lasting conditions for peace within two or three years.

Mayor's Declaration was different from past elaborations of the right to peace in that it not only confirmed the importance of peace as the precursor of all other rights, but also laid out a strategy to achieve it. The plan called for energies to be refocused on the systemic and root causes of conflict so that conflicts can be tackled in the early stages and the kind of out-of-control bloodletting that had characterized recent conflicts may be avoided.

Of course, to achieve the right to peace, it is first necessary to make the transition from a culture of war to a culture of peace. Mayor's Declaration realizes that the international community cannot simultaneously absorb the cost of war and the cost of peace. The Declaration is thus a wake-up call of sorts in that it puts the spotlight on a dangerously flawed international order and calls upon us to do what is necessary to build a more peaceful one. Not only is this necessary for our very survival, but since peace is "a prerequisite for the exercise of all human rights and duties," it is also our right.

The means to achieve this right are divided in the Declaration into two concurrent strategies. First, the Declaration calls for immediate action on urgent issues such as poverty, environmental destruction, and international justice, and it calls upon the international community to provide the UN system with the necessary resources and power to tackle these challenges. In other words, countries need to reduce their investment in arms and militarism and reinvest in the construction of peace. The second strategy involves a massive education campaign focused on youth and designed to foster an understanding and tolerance of other cultures as well as an understanding of the value of peace and justice.

In hindsight, and especially in the wake of September 11, these goals and their suggested timeline seem perhaps overly optimistic. But the Declaration nonetheless ignited a flurry of interest and activity among governments and civil society. It was quickly followed in 1997 by a meeting of experts organized by the University of Las Palmas, the Tricontinental Institute of Parliamentary Democracy and Human Rights, and UNESCO that was held in Las Palmas, Spain. The participants included Mohammed Bedjaoui, President of the International Court of Justice. The meeting recognized the intimate link between peace and human rights and called for a formal Declaration on the Human

Right to Peace, which would be ready for the 50th anniversary of the Universal Declaration on Human Rights in 1998.

The Oslo Draft Declaration

In 1997, the Norwegian Institute of Human Rights convened a meeting in Oslo to prepare a draft Declaration for UNESCO's General Conference later that year. The aim of the Declaration was to broaden the human dimension of peace and to divide the right to peace into three interrelated components. The first defines peace as a human right, understanding that all human beings have a right to peace inherent to their humanity. War and violence of any kind, including insecurity, are considered "intrinsically incompatible" with the human right to peace. The section calls on states and members of the international community to ensure its implementation without discrimination.

The second section elaborates on this task by making it a "duty" for all global actors, including individuals, to "contribute to the maintenance and construction of peace" and to prevent armed conflicts and prevent violence in all its manifestations.

The third section elaborates the "Culture of Peace"— the means by which the right to peace is to be achieved. As we have seen, the culture of peace is a strategy that seeks to root peace in peoples' minds through education, communication, and a set of ethical and democratic ideals.

Draft Oslo Declaration on the Human Right to Peace

Article 1: Peace as a human right

• Every human being has the right to peace, which is inherent in the dignity of the human person. War and all other armed conflicts, violence in all its forms and whatever its origin, and insecurity also, are intrinsically incompatible with the human right to peace;

• The human right to peace must be guaranteed, respected and implemented without any discrimination in either internal or international contexts by all states and other members of the international community;

Article 2: Peace as a duty

• Every human being, all states and other members of the international community and all peoples have the duty to contribute to the maintenance and construction of peace, and to the prevention of armed conflicts and of violence in all its forms. It is incumbent upon them notably to favour disarmament and to oppose by all legitimate means acts of aggression and systematic, massive and flagrant violations of human rights which constitute a threat to peace;

• As inequalities, exclusion and poverty can result in the disruption of peace both at the international level and internally, it is the duty of states to promote and encourage social justice both on their own territory and at the international level, in particular through an appropriate policy aimed at sustainable human development;

Article 3: Peace through the culture of peace

• The culture of peace, whose aim is to build the defences of peace in the minds of human beings every day through education, science and communication, must constitute the means of achieving the global implementation of the human right to peace;

• The culture of peace requires recognition and respect for – and the daily practice of – a set of ethical values and democratic ideals which are based on the intellectual and moral solidarity of humanity.

In essence, the right to peace is a global ethic of non-violence and reverence for all life and offers a blueprint for identifying the roots of global problems and for addressing conflicts early. It is an attempt to move beyond the day-to-day crises that make the headline news and to address their deep-seated causes.

The power of this draft declaration is in its challenge to the hypocrisy dominating the world order today, and it was here that the codification of the right to peace came to a temporary halt. A remarkable debate on the Oslo Draft Declaration took place in UNESCO's General Conference on November 6, 1997. One European country after another either attacked or expressed reservations about the right to peace and accused Mayor of overstepping his mandate. Countries from the South struck back, accusing the North of wanting to protect their arms industries. At the end, Paraguay stated, "This rich discussion shows that the culture of peace is the central issue ... and that the Human Right to Peace is needed for individuals and states." Noting that the debate split North and South, Paraguay added, "Perhaps peace is a greater concern in the South where scarce resources are being diverted to war."

Failing to achieve a consensus, Mayor did not press further with the issue. Skepticism about the human right to peace continued to echo for years after. In the informal discussions at the UN in 1999 that concerned the Draft Declaration and Programme of Action on a Culture of Peace, the US delegate stated, "Peace should not be elevated to the category of human right, otherwise it will be very difficult to start a war." Whether the speaker was aware of the irony of this statement or not, he had put his finger precisely on why a human right to peace is needed.

Efforts are continuing at the UN, but they still lack the necessary Western backing. In 2002, the UN Social, Humanitarian and Cultural Committee adopted a resolution calling for the promotion of the right to peace. (See box beginning on page 132.) The resolution would have the UN affirm that the peoples of the planet have a sacred right to peace, and resources released through disarmament measures should be devoted to the economic and social development of all peoples, particularly those in developing countries. Although the resolution had 90 votes in favour, a hefty 50 negative votes (mostly Western countries and the new East European members of NATO) were cast against it, and 14 abstentions were registered. Such division renders the resolution practically inoperable.

Some states are still arguing that the "right to peace" has not been negotiated at a sufficiently high level of international relations. Denmark, speaking for the European Union, said the issue should be dealt with in other forums (the same argument that was used in UNESCO meetings). Canada—speaking on behalf of the US, New Zealand, and Australia—expressed opposition because the resolution focused more on relations between states, as opposed to states' obligations to their peoples. The fact that Cuba was the main sponsor alienated many Western states. Nonetheless, an objective reading of the text does not provide any reason for rejection—unless a state wants to keep its options for warfare open. If the peoples of the states that voted against the resolution knew what their governments were doing, the governments would not be able to slide away so easily from their responsibility to build the structural basis for the right to peace.

When language is softer, the idea of moving away from war as a means of resolving conflict meets less resistance. For example, in 2003, the UN General Assembly concluded five months of negotiations by adopting by consensus a resolution on the prevention of armed conflict. The resolution called on parties to a dispute threatening international peace to make the most effective use of existing and new methods for peacefully settling disputes, including arbitration, mediation, other treaty-based arrangements, and the

International Criminal Court, thus promoting the role of international law in international relations. It reaffirmed the primary responsibility of the Security Council for the maintenance of international peace and security. And it called on Member States to support poverty eradication measures and enhance the capacity of developing countries; to comply with treaties on arms control, non-proliferation and disarmament; and to strengthen their international verification instruments and eradicate illicit trade in small arms and light weapons. The resolution was hailed as a landmark in efforts to move the world body from a culture of reacting to crises to one of preventing them reaching critical mass.

Though shying away from any implication that the prevention of armed conflict sets the stage for a full-scale discussion of the "right to peace," the resolution contains within it important elements of the culture of peace. Far from being anodyne or just another resolution, it is infused with an obligation to the victims of violence and challenges states to move from rhetoric to reality in preventing violence. It is a significant step forward by the UN in preparing the way for the right to peace.

Promotion of the Right of Peoples to Peace

The General Assembly...

1. *Reaffirms* the solemn proclamation that the peoples of our planet have a sacred right to peace;

2. *Solemnly declares* that the preservation of the right of peoples to peace and the promotion of its implementation constitute a fundamental obligation of each State;

3. *Emphasizes* that ensuring the exercise of the right of peoples to peace demands that the policies of States be directed towards the elimination of the threat of war, particularly nuclear war, the renunciation of the use or threat of use of force in international relations and the settlement of international disputes by peaceful means on the basis of the Charter of the United Nations;

4. *Affirms* that all States should promote the establishment, maintenance and strengthening of international peace and security and, to that end, should do their utmost to achieve general and complete disarmament under effective international control, as well as to ensure that the resources released by effective disarmament measures are used for comprehensive development, in particular that of the developing countries;

5. *Urges* the international community to devote part of the resources made available by the implementation of disarmament and arms limitation agreements to economic and social development, with a view to reducing the ever-widening gap between developed and developing countries, and to promote the realization of all human rights for all;

6. *Urges* all States to refrain from using weapons with indiscriminate effects on human health, the environment and economic and social well-being;

7. *Expresses concern* at the real danger of the weaponization of outer space, and calls upon all States to contribute actively to the objective of the peaceful use of outer space and of the prevention of an arms race in outer space;

8.   *Urges* all States to refrain from taking measures which encourage the resurgence of a new arms race, bearing in mind all the resulting predictable consequences for global peace and security, for development and for the full realization of all human rights for all;

9.   *Decides* to continue its consideration of the promotion of the rights of peoples to peace at its fifty-eighth session, under the item entitled human rights questions.

Meanwhile, attention in UNESCO has shifted back from a right to peace to the culture of peace. This was easier to digest for those who did not want their right to make war impeded. Everyone, after all, could be for peace in general, and especially in the abstract. UNESCO showed its wisdom by treading slowly. It developed the concept of the culture of peace into a series of programs that would, at least in the minds of those who truly understood the dimensions of the culture of peace, prepare the groundwork for a later acceptance of the human right to peace.

A Third Generation of Rights

To fully grasp the potential of the human right to peace to change human conduct, it is necessary to consider the evolving nature of human rights.

"First generation" political and civil human rights emanated from the American and French Revolutions in an effort to protect the liberty of the individual from the tyranny and abuse of the state. "Second generation" economic, social, and cultural rights were products of the Mexican and Russian Revolutions opposing unjust social inequality. A "third generation" of rights is developing as a product of the urgent problems of globalization that characterize the world today. Both the first and second generations were essentially about the role of the state vis-à-vis the individual. The first generation of human rights revolved around the "rights of" individuals to exercise certain civil and political liberties free from state interference, and the second generation of human rights were individual "rights to" economic and social equality provided by the state.

The third generation of human rights is unique in that these rights cannot be realized simply through actions of governments; they require the symbiotic co-operation between people and states. Karl Vasak, the human rights scholar who is credited with initiating the concept of third generation human rights, describes them in these terms:

> [They] are new in the aspirations they express, are new from the point of view of human rights in that they seek to infuse the human dimension into areas where it has all too often been missing, having been left to the State, or States. ...They are new in that they may both be *invoked against* the State *and demanded of it*; but above all (and herein lies their essential characteristic) *they can be realized only through the concerted efforts of all actors on the social scene:* the individual, the State, public and private bodies and the *international community*.

Essentially, third generation rights call for the redistribution of power and resources, and consider the current international system ineffective in its attempts to resolve contemporary issues. Third generation rights include: the right to political, economic, and cultural self-determination; the right to economic and social development; the right to participate in and benefit from the common heritage of mankind; the right to a healthy environment; the right to humanitarian relief; and the right to peace. The key characteristic of these rights is that they are fundamentally collective in nature and require international co-operation for their achievement. A clean environment cannot be achieved by the actions of one country, since pollution does not recognize national frontiers.

Likewise, it is difficult for a country to raise its gross national product when other countries' tariffs prevent it from selling its goods to raise revenue that could be put toward social services.

More generally, third generation rights provide an essential ingredient lacking in first and second generation rights. Largely based on the individual, first and second generation rights are permeated by an atmosphere of selfishness that sees the individual as the primary concern. But this focus neglects the fact that, more than ever, society is a system of competing groups and individuals and that, for society to achieve its full potential, it is necessary to participate co-operatively within the community. Achieving this demands major changes from the individualistic attitude that prevails in Western democracies.

The challenges inherent in globalization make such an approach vitally necessary. The very nature of the dilemmas the third generation of rights seeks to address—namely the right to a clean environment, development, and peace—are issues that today pertain to humanity's very survival. The world has rapidly compressed through a breathtaking combination of population growth, technological and economic advancement, and interdependence. Combining these with a readily available supply of deadly weapons and easily transmitted contagion of hatred and incitement to violence makes it essential and urgent to find ways to prevent disputes from turning massively violent.

In reality, more than a new generation, third generation rights are perhaps better thought of as an awakening. World problems can no longer be solved by the actions of one state alone. Keeping the peace, protecting the environment, and fostering sustained and equitable development require co-operative and determined action at the international level. Lacking this, states cannot fulfill their first and second generational obligations.

Human rights are thus indivisible and interdependent. One set of human rights cannot be realized in a world where others are absent or violated. Framed this way, the metaphor for successive "generations" of rights is somewhat misleading since, although they coexist, generations actually succeed each other in the true sense of the term. In reality, the international community has approached human rights in a top-down fashion. Just as it was realized that taking the first generation of human rights seriously necessitated fulfilling the second, achieving the first and second generations of human rights in a globalized world requires realizing the third set of rights. Although at a nascent stage and thus not as established as its "ancestors," this new generation of rights offers a blueprint for confronting and managing the pressing challenges posed by globalization.

The most important among these newly emerging rights is the human right to peace. Often regarded as just another third generation right in the human rights literature, the right to peace is unique. It transcends all other rights, enables their exercise, and offers the innovation needed to lift up society and allow it to achieve its full potential in an interconnected world. Indeed, without basic security of the person, other human rights are but an illusion. What use is the right to vote, or the right to medical care, in a society torn apart by armed conflict?

Answering the Critics

Some critics have turned these arguments around. In his book *Human Rights and Peace*, David P. Forsythe argues that there is no such thing as a right to peace since it has "no specific meaning" and offers no idea of "specific duties." As evidence, he points out that, unlike its first and second generation counterparts, the right to peace and other third generation rights have never been formalized into a legal treaty, much less specific legal rules. He goes on to state that this new generation of rights is really only political rhetoric and has never reached the stage of constituting legal obligations on governments. The human rights scholar and advocate Paul Sieghart is even more absolute in arguing that it is difficult to see how third generation rights can be called human rights at all, since only rights of human individuals can be true "human" rights. This line of argument holds that third generation rights, due to their international dimension, cannot be secured by law and that, by trying to expand the human rights regime in such a way, we risk diluting "truer" rights.

Although sympathetic to international human rights in principle, Forsythe concludes that they must have independent meaning and set down specific behaviour that is permissible and impermissible. Third generation rights— including the rights to peace, development, and a clean environment—are seen as "synthetic or composite rights, drawn from other recognized rights and used to emphasize or educate or socialize" and useful as "political devices" only. Using the right to peace as an example, Forsythe considers it a rehashing of *jus ad bellum*, the rules for recourse to force, another well-established body of international law. According to him, since *jus ad bellum* already addresses concepts like anticipatory self-defence, intervention, armed attack, individual and collective self-defence, and expanded self-defence (including reprisals), focusing too much on a right to peace only leads to redundancy. He says much the same of any right to development, calling the very term development amorphous and the UN's definition of it as "mumbo jumbo par excellence."

At the very least, Forsythe's criticism is stagnant in its view and offers little to move the human rights regime forward and adapt it to the contemporary international system. Forsythe allows that first and second generation rights have evolved to the point where they are meaningful, but does not afford the same potential to third generation rights, since they have not been "formalized into legal principles" and have no "independent and specific meaning." The fact is, international human rights law is dynamic, and even the most rooted human rights have been developed and introduced into international law only gradually.

Human rights are a product of their times, and such is the case with first and second generation rights. One group of rights is not meant to outdate or ascend another, but rather to expand upon and supplement others. This is clear in the international community's continually expanding conception of what it considers to be human rights and the strides that have been made to formalize them. New aspects of life, new situations, and new types of conflict that cannot be foreseen are continually pushing the definition of human rights beyond old limits. This is a normal legal process that has been adopted by national legal systems the world over, and it should be no surprise that the same process is becoming evident in an increasingly interconnected world.

Such is the case with the right to peace, which is the product of a paradigm shift at the international level. Rights that focus solely on the relationship between the state and the individual are not sufficient in responding to a globalized world in which problems are no longer defined purely in national terms. The same global circuitry that fuels transportation, information, finance, and organization has also increased the power of the arms trader, the warlord, the religious fanatic, the deranged political leader, the human trafficker, and the terrorist. There is, thus, a technological burden with which the other two generations of human rights were never designed to cope, and the right to peace is an attempt to respond to the perils of the modern interconnected world. Dismissing the right to peace as vague and declaring that it offers nothing new is an exercise that misses the mark. The right to peace is innovative and addresses a whole swath of new and interconnected global challenges.

Obviously, the world community has much work to do before the "right to peace" is codified in the same way that political, civil, economic, and social rights have been codified in the covenants to the Universal Declaration of Human Rights. But the fact that so much progress has been made in recognizing, defining, and implementing the right to peace is a sign of the advance of civilization. Those who wish to maintain the war culture and divert yet more precious resources to prosecute wars must not be permitted to use the terrorist attacks of September 11 as an excuse. This will not get at the systemic causes of the problems faced by the international community today.

Only when we fully understand our own potential to make the human right to peace the ruling norm in society will the international community have fulfilled the promise it made in 1945. This promise was to construct the defences of peace in the minds of all the peoples of the Earth and finally "save succeeding generations from the scourge of war."

"Human Rights Have Come a Long Way"

In considering the difficulties of enshrining the human right to peace in law, it is helpful to consider the overall progress made on the human rights agenda. The whole field of human rights has taken centre stage starting with the Universal Declaration and followed by the covenants; the various conventions on women's and children's rights; and such instruments as the Anti-Personnel Landmines Treaty, the Rwanda and Yugoslav tribunals, and the International Court of Justice. As Mary Robinson, former UN High Commissioner for Human Rights (and former President of Ireland), puts it: "Human rights have indeed come a long way." Even though many governments do not necessarily observe human rights standards, most at least acknowledge that human rights have a role to play.

There is no question that the development process was spurred by the UN's assertion in 1986 of the "Right to Development." A resolution adopted that year stated firmly:

> The right to development is an inalienable human right by virtue of which every human person and all peoples are entitled to participate in, contribute to, and enjoy economic, social, cultural and political development, in which all human rights and fundamental freedoms can be fully realized.

The resolution emphasized that "the human person is the central subject of development," and inspired development planners who then began to place more emphasis on education and health in funding development projects. The resolution stated that elimination of threats of war would enhance the development process and that resources released by disarmament should be devoted to the economic and social development of peoples. This contributed significantly to an understanding that development requires the presence of peace, and peace cannot endure without the conditions of development.

The Declaration on the Right to Development and the Declaration on the Right of Peoples to Peace (adopted during the same time period) broaden the basis of human rights to consider both peace and development. Both underscore the key idea that all human rights are "indivisible and interdependent." Human rights are inherent in each human being. They are not conferred by the state, but states do have the obligation to uphold and enforce the application of human rights.

Like the right to peace, the right to development is criticized because it cannot be enforced. When is a person "developed"? When is there "peace"? These objections are invalid, since the declaration of rights, carried out with the consensus of humanity through international institutions, is meant to set norms for human conduct. These norms, at their extreme end, can be enforced. The state has an obligation to provide food to a starving child. The state has an obligation to protect civilians during warfare. Only when more sophisticated interpretations of rights are called for does consensus begin to break down. How much Official Development Assistance should be provided by a state to help developing countries? At what point does a state's level of weaponry exceed its needs for defence and become a threat to its neighbour? These questions, the stuff of the political process, must be dealt with on a daily basis. Ongoing debates must stand on principles, and those principles are expressed in the human rights conventions.

The essence of this responsibility was encapsulated by the World Conference on Human Rights in Vienna in 1993, which asserted:

> All human rights are universal, indivisible and interdependent and interrelated. The international community must treat human rights globally in a fair and equal manner, on the same footing, and with the same emphasis. While the significance of national and regional particularities and various historical, cultural and religious backgrounds must be borne in mind, it is the duty of States, regardless of their political, economic and cultural systems, to promote and protect all human rights and fundamental freedoms.

The forward-minded nature of the UN's work on the delineation and implementation of human rights is seen particularly in the Convention on the Rights of the Child. The Convention is a universally agreed upon set of non-negotiable standards and obligations. It spells out the basic human rights that children everywhere, without discrimination, have. These are the right to survival; to develop to the fullest; to protection from harmful influences, abuse, and exploitation; and to participate fully in family, cultural, and social life. The Convention protects children's rights by setting standards in health care and in education, legal, civil, and social services. These standards are benchmarks against which progress can be assessed. States that are parties to the Convention are obliged to develop and undertake actions and policies in the best interests of the child.

The Convention on the Rights of the Child is the first legally binding international instrument to incorporate the full range of human rights—civil and political rights as well as economic, social, and cultural rights. Two Optional Protocols to strengthen the Convention entered into force in 2002; these address the involvement of children in armed conflict, the sale of children, child prostitution, and child pornography. The Convention is the most universally accepted human rights instrument in history. It uniquely places children at the forefront in the quest for the universal application of human rights. By ratifying this instrument, national governments have committed themselves to protecting and ensuring children's rights, and they have agreed to hold themselves accountable before the international community. Every country in the world has ratified it except two: the US and Somalia.

In considering to what the child is entitled so that he or she can live in minimum economic and social standards, is it too much of a leap to state that the first thing the child needs to grow up safely is a peaceful environment? Children must have peace in order to develop in a way that is consistent with the inherent human rights they possess. Peace is their right. But it cannot yet be formally articulated in ways that guarantee that the processes of sustainable development will not be destroyed by the ravages of war. The political system has not yet sufficiently matured.

Nonetheless, the subject of the human right to peace has clearly entered circles of discussion at the UN. Some hold that it is already a component of developing international law. This is a signal moment because a full discussion of the right to peace puts a new spotlight on the age-old question of the abolition of war itself. In the new era of weapons of mass destruction, the viability of war as a legal means to resolve disputes is clearly over. War today can lead to the obliteration of humanity. Unfortunately, the world community, held in check by the forces of the culture of war, is a long way from outlawing war. The debate on the human right to peace, therefore, is a step forward. As it is pursued, it will force the political system to face up to its responsibility to at least avoid war.

The debate inevitably will centre on the deeply controversial question of the future of nuclear weapons. The International Court of Justice has already given its view on this matter: it says nations have a legal obligation to get rid of them. While the abolition of nuclear weapons will not by itself guarantee peace, it is an elementary fact of the twenty-first century that as long as nations brandish nuclear weapons there can be no peace. Indeed, P.N. Bhagwati, former Chief Justice of the Supreme Court of India, argues that "the main function of the right to peace is the promotion and protection of the right to life through peaceful settlement of disputes, by the prohibition of the threat or use of force in international relations, by the prohibition of the manufacture, use and deployment of nuclear weapons, and by total disarmament."

The proponents of nuclear weapons do indeed know which way the debate on the human right to peace is headed. That is why they will use every argument they can think of, every political device they can find, and every form of intimidation they can invent to try to derail the debate. They effectively disrupted the debate in UNESCO. They have rendered inoperative nuclear weapons abolition resolutions at the UN. They have used the tragedy of September 11 to scare the populace into believing that only gigantic amounts of weaponry can head off the terrorism of the future. They have already caused an erosion of civil liberties in the guise of combating terrorism.

These proponents of militarism as the route to peace appear to operate today from the commanding heights of public opinion. But against this insidious thinking that war equals peace is rising a new army—not of soldiers but of highly informed, dedicated, and courageous citizens of all countries who do see the perils ahead. There is a blossoming of both understanding and action in the new phenomenon of an alert civil society calling governments to account for paying only lip service to their human rights commitments. Buttressed by the dynamic means of electronic communication, they are bringing new energy to the global quest for peace. Much of that energy is flowing through the UN system, to which I now turn.

6

The United Nations:
Making Haste Slowly

If enshrining the human right to peace appears to be some distance off, the themes of the culture of peace are very much within reach, and there is no better instrument to bring this about than the UN. The terrorism of September 11, 2001, and the wars in Afghanistan and Iraq have brought about a new period of fear, confusion, and loss of a sense of direction. In this world, the best response to today's heightened vulnerability is for the UN to step up its life-saving work around the world: preventing and containing conflict, eliminating weapons of mass destruction, fighting poverty, reducing hunger, improving health care, defending human rights, protecting the environment, and promoting democracy.

Humanity needs a new way to express and fulfill its longing for true human security, and the UN offers the blueprint. Begun in 1945, the UN has had only a short time, historically speaking, in which to accomplish a transition from the culture of war mentality to the culture of peace. Taking a long-range view of world affairs, it is clear that the UN is still in its infancy. The focus should be on what it has accomplished and can accomplish, rather than on what it has not. The UN is pilloried because it failed to stop the genocidal massacres in Rwanda in 1994 and Srebrenica in 1995. But it is seldom credited with averting bloodshed in Lebanon, Georgia, Western Sahara, the Ivory Coast, and many other places through its skillful use of negotiation and mediation. The UN has saved countless lives through developing and distributing affordable medicines, improving water supplies, and providing sanitation methods. It has put the inherent dignity of each individual at the top of the international agenda. It has provided a catalogue of information on the interdependence of world systems never before available.

More international law has been developed through the UN in the past five decades than in the entire previous history of humankind. The UN is the depository of 429 major and enforceable multilateral instruments. These treaties provide a framework for legal norms spanning a spectrum of human interactions in war and peace. The UN formulated the Universal Declaration on Human Rights and 80 instruments to protect and promote specific human rights. The UN has strengthened the democratic process by monitoring elections in some 80 countries. It promoted the great movement of decolonization, which led to the independence of scores of nations. The UN defines technical standards in telecommunication, aviation, shipping, and postal services, which make international transactions possible. It increasingly engages in joint ventures with the private sector and international organizations, such as a project to provide continuous web-accessed satellite imagery, image-processing devices, maps, and other geographic information to assist UN agencies and NGOs providing humanitarian assistance or carrying out post-conflict rehabilitation and recon-struction projects. Its intergovernmental character gives the UN practical advantages in high-level diplomacy that are not always available to individual governments.

The UN's potential to build the conditions for peace was seen in the General Assembly's unanimous adoption of the McCloy-Zorin Accords in 1961, which, had the document endured, would have buried the culture of war. US President John F. Kennedy and Soviet President Nikita Khrushchev instructed their principal arms control negotiators, John J. McCloy and Valerian Zorin, to negotiate a framework for comprehensive disarmament. In five months, the American and Soviet teams produced a historic document that committed the two superpowers to negotiate an agreement to "ensure that disarmament is general and complete and war is no longer an instrument for settling international problems." The vision of disarmament embraced by the negotiators was more comprehensive than anything found today. It was nothing less than general and complete disarmament—including disbanding armed forces, dismantling military establishments, and eliminating stockpiles of nuclear, chemical, biological, and other weapons of mass destruction. An International Disarmament Organization run by the UN was to oversee effective verification. The UN would have an international peace force to "effectively deter or suppress any threat or use of arms in violation of the purpose and principles of the UN." Viewed in the hindsight of the cold and hot wars of the past four decades, and in the context of today's reassertion of militarism, the McCloy-Zorin Accords are astounding.

However, the Accords were pushed aside by divisions caused by the Berlin Wall, the Cuban Missile Crisis, the Vietnam War, and the assassination of President Kennedy. They did give birth to the Eighteen-Nation Disarmament Committee, which became the present-day Conference on Disarmament. For one brief shining moment, it looked like an era of peace could be built with the UN as the centre of world activity.

Chief Forum for the Culture of Peace

The UN is our best hope to build the conditions for peace and provide human security for everyone. World peace will not come through governments, military alliances, corporations, or the powerful institutions that dominate daily life. They have not brought peace in the past. Why should we expect them to do so in the future?

The UN's central purpose is to maintain international peace and security. It is, therefore, important to consider it as the chief forum to promote and implement the culture of peace. Let us look again at elements necessary for the culture of peace.

The Programme of Action on a Culture of Peace, adopted by the UN General Assembly in 1999, includes these elements:

• Educating everyone, with improved curricula to improve training in dialogue, consensus-building, conflict prevention, and crisis management

• Increasing international co-operation to reduce poverty and external debt, and increase the food supply

• Strengthening national work to implement the full range of human rights described in the Vienna Declaration of 1993

• Promoting equality between women and men in economic, social, and political decision-making and making special efforts to eliminate all forms of discrimination and violence against women

• Training public officials and providing electoral assistance to sustain democracy

• Combating terrorism, organized crime, corruption, and trafficking in illicit drugs

• Supporting tolerance and solidarity throughout society with special attention to refugees, migrants, and displaced persons

• Making effective use of the media and the Internet to share information on peace-building

- Promoting general and complete disarmament under strict and effective international control, as called for by the UN, with special attention to ending the traffic in small arms

- Refraining from military coercion and minimizing the humanitarian impact of sanctions on women and children

- Promoting days of tranquillity to deliver medicine, immunize people, and ensure delivery of humanitarian supplies.

Kofi Annan's Vision

The agenda of the UN embraces each of these steps. Secretary-General Kofi Annan, the Ghanaian diplomat educated in the US, whose whole career has been spent in the UN system, personifies an artful and dexterous form of leadership in trying to implement this agenda. Considering that the Secretary-General of the UN has no practical political power, it is remarkable that he has been so influential. As *The New Yorker* commented, "He controls no territory; he commands no troops; he cannot make or enforce laws; he cannot levy taxes; he exercises no administrative authority outside the UN bureaucracy, and he hasn't even got a vote in its General Assembly or the Security Council." To put it plainly, the Secretary-General has nothing but his voice.

Annan and the UN were awarded the 2001 Nobel Peace Prize. Annan led the Millennium celebrations at the UN with a special summit of world leaders for which he prepared a stirring document: *We the Peoples: The Role of the United Nations in the Twenty-first Century*. Make globalization a positive force for all the world's people, he said, instead of leaving billions of them behind in squalor. "We must do more than talk about our future, however. We must start to create it now." The leaders responded with a UN Millennium Declaration built on "fundamental values" for the twenty-first century: freedom, equality, solidarity, tolerance, respect for nature, and shared responsibility.

Almost exactly a year after the Declaration was adopted, this message of UN values received a defiant and horrifying rebuff in the September 11 attacks. Since then, tensions have escalated throughout the world and finally boiled over with the start of the war against Iraq. Instead of moving toward the goals of the Declaration, the world seems to be slipping into more conflict. This is precisely why, as the Secretary-General has said repeatedly, the UN's multilateral efforts to maintain international peace and security must be reinforced. "We have entered the third millennium through a gate of fire," Annan said in his speech accepting the Nobel Peace Prize. "If today, after the horror of September 11, we see better and we see further – we will realize that humanity is indivisible. We must start from the understanding that peace belongs not only to states or peoples, but to each and every member of those communities."

If ever fully implemented, the Millennium Declaration would make the world a peaceful (and pleasant) place. However, when it came to paying the bill to implement these values, leaders coughed and sputtered. They did, however, agree to a set of Millennium Development Goals setting targets for combating poverty, hunger, disease, illiteracy, environmental degradation, and discrimination against women by the year 2015 (see box on pages 151-153). The key to achieving the goals is an effective global partnership for development between the developed and developing countries, but such a partnership is still in the embryonic stage. Not only must the rich double their aid to reach the goals, the poor countries themselves must put the Millennium Goals at the centre of their development strategy.

Though rebuffed on money, Annan is trying to make progress by integrating the goals in all aspects of the UN's work at the country level and setting up a global monitoring system. The aim is to galvanize public opinion to boost development assistance, trade, debt relief, technology, and other support needed to achieve the goals.

Well aware that governments, left to themselves, will never implement a human security agenda, Annan adroitly convened an extraordinary meeting of 1,350 representatives of 100 non-governmental organizations (NGOs) from 145 countries a few months before the summit of government leaders. For five days, delegates focused on the role of the UN and civil society in peace, poverty eradication, human rights, the environment, globalization, and the revitalization of the UN. The delegates issued a Declaration and Agenda for Action that called for a Global Poverty Eradication Fund, a Global Habitat Conservation Fund, a UN Peace Force, and a UN Humanitarian Commission. The Forum's leader, Techeste Ahderom, the main representative of the Baha'i International Community to the United Nations, brought the Declaration to the government summit. In it, the NGO group resolved "to create a global civil society forum as a permanent forum to deal with UN institutions, the UN reform process, member states and other institutions."

The Millennium Development Goals

The Millennium Development Goals (MDGs) are contained in the Millennium Declaration adopted by the United Nations Millennium Summit in September 2000. They are a refinement of the International Development Goals and are derived from the agreements and resolutions of United Nations conferences in the 1990s. They consist of the following eight goals:

1. *Eradicate extreme poverty and hunger.*

   - Halve the proportion of people whose income is less than one dollar a day by year 2015

   - Halve the proportion of people who suffer from hunger by year 2015.

---

2. *Attain universal primary education in all countries by year 2015*:

    • Ensure children of both sexes everywhere will be able to complete a full course of primary schooling.

3. *Promote gender equality and empower women*:

    • Eliminate gender disparity in primary and secondary education, preferably by the year 2005, and at all levels of education no later that 2015.

4. *Reduce child mortality*:

    • Reduce by two-thirds under-five mortality rate by 2015.

5. *Improve maternal health*:

    • Reduce by three-quarters the maternal mortality rate by year 2015.

6. *Combat HIV/AIDS, malaria, and other diseases*:

    • Halt by 2015, and begin to reverse the spread of HIV/AIDS

    • Halt by 2015, and begin to reverse the incidence of malaria and other major diseases.

7. *Ensure Environmental sustainability*:

    • Integrate the principles of sustainable development into country policies and programs and reverse the loss of environmental resources

    • Halve by 2015 the proportion of people without access to safe drinking water

    • Achieve a significant improvement in the lives of at least 100 million slum dwellers by 2020.

8. *Develop a global partnership for development*:

    • Develop further an open rule-based, predictable, non-discriminatory trading and financial system

    • Address the special needs of the least developed countries

    • Address the special needs of landlocked countries and small island developing states

- Deal comprehensively with the debt problems of developing countries through national and international measures in order to make debt sustainable in the long term

- In cooperation with developing countries, develop and implement strategies for decent and productive work for youth

- In cooperation with pharmaceutical companies, provide access to affordable essential drugs in developing countries

- In cooperation with the private sector, make available the benefits of new technologies, especially information and communications.

The Declaration and Agenda for Action show clearly how far ahead of government the advanced wing of civil society is moving. "The UN and its member states have failed to fulfill their primary responsibility of maintaining peace and preserving human life. Organized armed violence is depriving millions of people all over the world – 95 per cent of them civilians – of their lives, and many millions more of their right to peace." The statement criticized the fact that no decisive progress had been made to eliminate nuclear weapons in more than 50 years. The delegates called for a special session of the UN General Assembly on disarmament. They recommended the creation of a Global Poverty Eradication Fund to ensure that the poor have access to credit. And they called for binding codes of conduct for transnational companies, as well as tax measures designed to support the UN and other international institutions. To develop additional revenue sources for the UN, the group suggested fees for the commercial use of the oceans and skies, and a tax on the carbon content of fuels. The UN should be further strengthened, they said, with a parliamentary assembly made up of elected legislators. Such a strengthening of the UN is certainly far off in a foggy future. But just as it took vision to start the UN, it takes vision to develop its architecture so that the UN will have at least a fair chance to prove that it can develop a world that is human-centred and genuinely democratic, where all human beings are full participants in determining their own destinies.

So Much with So Little

It is time to stop taking the UN for granted and to stop attacking the organization for its failures, which is a sort of sport played by biased and often uninformed commentators. Governments must also stop starving the UN of funds, which major governments do deliberately out of fear the UN will become too powerful.

That the UN can do so much with so little money is amazing and deserves the appreciation of the world. Its regular budget is only $1.3 billion per year, which pays for a basic infrastructure and staff of 8,900 employees, drawn from virtually all 191 member countries, who work in the principal UN centres of New York, Geneva, Vienna, and Nairobi. All official meetings and documentation require interpretation and translation into its six official languages— English and French (the two working languages), Spanish, Russian, Chinese, and Arabic. The entire UN system, which includes peacekeeping operations and UN agencies, funds, and programs (such as the UN Development Programme, the World Food Programme, the UN Children's Fund, and the UN Population Fund), costs $12 billion a year. This is 1/70th the amount of annual world military expenditures.

Those who claim the UN is a bloated "talk shop" are either ignorant or mischievous. The budget for New York City's Board of Education for 2001 was more than $12.4 billion; the two states in the US with the smallest budgets— Wyoming and South Dakota—have a budget of more than $2 billion each (much more than the UN's administrative budget).

A mixture of assessments and voluntary contributions makes up the $12 billion. The primary criterion for the calculation of membership dues is a country's capacity to pay. The maximum assessment for the regular budget is 22 per cent, the minimum 0.01 per cent. This latter percentage is what the 43 least developed countries pay. Only one country, the US, is in the top category. When the US withheld its payments in the 1990s to protest certain UN activities, the organization was plunged into financial crisis. Because the US is the largest contributor, its action had the largest impact, but its default was not solitary. Some countries fail to pay their dues on time due to budgetary technicalities or simple poverty. Although the schedule of payments by the US and others has now improved and the UN has been saved from the worst of the crisis, no state or private company could function under such financial conditions.

In the wake of September 11, more and more is asked of the UN. But the paucity of funding for a global organization expressly designed to build the conditions of peace, which, if implemented, would save governments many times the amount they spend on warfare, is one of the great paradoxes of our time. This is not just a question of underfunding. Finances are a reflection of the prevailing problem of power structures, which are the very factors continuing to shore up the culture of war. Application of the culture of peace would, over the long run, diminish the impact of today's power structures by increasing the ability of citizenries around the world to control their own destinies. This work of true liberation cannot depend for its existence on the largesse—philosophical as well as financial—of the present power structures. It must find its way using routes that do not converge in the corridors of big governments. The UN opens up such routes, such as the global conferences it has held, which have spotlighted world problems, and the fostering of highly informed NGOs.

The UN depends on big governments; it could not exist without them. Therefore, it is always constricted by what they will allow. Although the UN Charter opens with the famous phrase "We the peoples of the United Nations ...," governments, not people, run the organization. As the Carnegie Commission on Preventing Deadly Conflict points out, "Many countries, including some of the most powerful, use the UN as a fig leaf and a smokescreen to blur unwanted focus, to defuse political pressure, or to dilute or evade their own responsibilities. States—again, even the most powerful —often make commitments that they fail to honour." Nations cannot repeatedly ignore the rule of law, bypass the UN, continue their recourse to the use of force, and then expect the institution—which they have weakened and damaged by their actions—to function effectively in solving problems. Governments, for the most part, still put their national interests first and only slowly are beginning to adapt their thinking to give a higher standing to the common good of humanity rather than to their own concerns.

The Role of the UN in Warfare

Agonizing questions about the role of the UN in a time of conflict are still unresolved. Should the UN authorize wars? Should the UN fight wars? How can it stand for the culture of peace if it engages in the culture of war? The 2003 conflict between the US and Iraq brought these questions to a head.

The Charter of the UN states, in Article 41, that the Security Council may impose sanctions against an aggressor state. If these prove to be inadequate to stop the aggression, the Security Council, under Article 42, may take military action to maintain or restore international peace. The UN took such military action in 1950 in sending troops to fight under the UN flag in Korea. That was the only time such action occurred until 1991, when the Security Council, under Resolution 678, authorized "all necessary means" to be taken against Iraq for its invasion of Kuwait. The death of at least 100,000 Iraqi soldiers and civilians in a UN-sanctioned, but US-led, war shocked many long-time UN supporters who felt that the US had manipulated the Security Council to push Resolution 678 through. The Secretary-General at the time, Javier Perez de Cuellar, was so concerned about the UN's reputation that he spoke out to try to clear the air. In an address to the European Parliament on April 18, 1991, he said: "The victory of the allied, or coalition, countries over Iraq is not at all a victory for the United Nations, because this was not its war. It was not a United Nations war."

Even though the Security Council was given no role in the prosecution of the war (in this sense, Perez de Cuellar was right), the fact that the UN had authorized the war laid the groundwork for what was to come. The US insisted on authorization to attack Afghanistan in the wake of September 11 and received it; the UN did not engage in the bombing attacks, but was left with the clean-up and then given little money to do it. When the US was determined to attack Iraq again in 2003, on the grounds that it had not followed Security Council resolutions ordering the destruction of its weapons of mass destruction, the Security Council balked.

It was one of the most dramatic moments in the UN's history. The US virtually demanded that it be given UN authorization to attack Iraq and said plainly that if it did not receive such a mandate it would attack anyway. France, along with Russia and Germany, held out for a continuation of the inspection process. Seeing that it was thwarted by the threatened French veto, and that it was running into walls trying to buy off weaker non-permanent members, the US struck. Having done the unthinkable—standing up to the US—the UN was then praised by those who opposed the Iraq war and condemned by those who either favoured or accepted war as the only way to depose Saddam Hussein.

It will take the world community considerable time to repair the damage and deep divisions running through the UN. The war had hardly begun when the UN was called on to provide humanitarian assistance, and alleviating human suffering became the foremost concern of the UN leadership. It might have been expected that the reconstruction of a post-Saddam government in Iraq would be entrusted to the UN. But so determined was the US to control all aspects of the new Iraq—including awarding lucrative contracts to American businesses—that it shoved the UN aside and put US appointees in charge. Many Islamic leaders, both inside and outside Iraq, protested against the continuing—at least for the time being—American presence.

The US resistance to putting the UN in charge of building a democratic government in post-war Iraq showed once more the reluctance of the powerful to give the UN the authority it needs to build peace in the world. The UN's job is not just to clean up *after* wars; it is to *prevent* them. The UN must not be reduced to an international welfare agency. The credibility and authority of the UN in stopping nations from warring with one another must be restored. The UN's role in building the basis for international law must be recognized as its primary function. The statement by Andrew Mack and Ramesh Thakur, two UN authorities, cannot be said often enough: "[The UN is] the indispensable font of international authority and the irreplaceable forum for authorizing international military enforcement."

We have not yet reached the level of civilization where all national governments will invest the UN with the authority it needs to fulfill the goals of its charter. But we must keep trying to strengthen the web of international law that offers the only hope of preserving a semblance of order in a globalized world. Just because the organization cannot prevent all wars does not invalidate its work of trying to do so. The work of achieving disarmament by peaceful means rather than war must go on. The millions around the world who marched for peace before and during the Iraq war, the hundreds of NGOs that spearheaded a ban on anti-personnel land mines, and the countries that fought tooth and nail to create the International Criminal Court will support this work.

Those who damn the UN as "irrelevant" in questions of war forget that the UN Charter does indeed permit the Security Council to authorize military action. Perez de Cuellar's successor as Secretary-General, Boutros Boutros-Ghali of Egypt, tried to strengthen the UN so that it—not an individual state—would have the tools to enforce peace. At the Security Council Summit of 1992, he was requested to produce recommendations for preventive diplomacy, peacemaking, and peacekeeping. At that time, the UN had achieved wide acclaim for its accomplishments in peacekeeping and had, in fact, received the 1988 Nobel Peace Prize for its peacekeeping work. But peacekeeping presumes at least a truce so that deployed troops can maintain, if not peace, then an absence of war.

With the end of the Cold War and the world heading into unchartered territory, Boutros-Ghali took a proactive stance for peace, and, in his remarkable document *An Agenda for Peace*, called on the UN to include "peacemaking" with its preventive diplomacy and peacekeeping work. He recommended a permanent UN force of "peace-enforcement units" authorized by the Security Council and under the command of the Secretary-General to be sent into a trouble spot to deter an aggressor. This means fighting. Boutros-Ghali foresaw that such units would not be sufficiently large or well enough equipped to deal with a major threat from an army equipped with sophisticated weapons. "They would be useful, however, in meeting any threat posed by a military force of a lesser order." His main argument for the need of such a force was to demonstrate "the credibility of the UN as a guarantor of international security." The issue of whether the UN should have its own permanent military force, however small, has not been settled. It needs much more examination in the light of the regional conflicts that have broken out in the post-Cold War years.

Of course, the *Agenda for Peace* was not accepted; both major and minor powers, for their own reasons, opposed what would be, in effect, a UN standing army that would both cost money and rival national power. But Boutros-Ghali performed a service in forcing the international community to face up to the essential question of just how to enforce peace. Some important states, notably France and Canada, do favour a UN rapid deployment force. If such a force had been in existence from the beginning, it is conceivable that numerous conflicts could have been quickly defused before they erupted into serious violence. For the UN to show its presence in situations of potential aggression is valuable. Nonetheless, some hold that the overarching job of the UN is to keep the peace, and not legitimize or authorize (let alone make) war under any circumstances.

Just as the police in a local community are called upon to "enforce" peace even to the extent of sacrificing their lives against murderers, so too the culture of peace and the right to peace require an enforcement mechanism at the international level. We have begun to build such instruments: Articles 41 and 42 and related sections of the UN Charter; the International Court of Justice; the new International Criminal Court; and the work done on humanitarian intervention. If the right to peace is inherent in all humans— and I argue that this is the case—then it must be guaranteed globally under the same principle as laws applied at the local level. The peace in my community is not impaired but is helped by the presence of the local police. This does not mean that it is only the enforcement powers of the local police that are necessary for peace; a wide range of economic and social measures lie at the root of peace in my community.

Alternatives to Militarism

Of course, developing alternatives to military intervention is far better. That is what the culture of peace is all about. But unless the international community, through the UN, comes to an agreement on the development of a military force under the direct control of the Security Council, we will see the major powers continue to wage war when they deem it in their interests to do so. As long as each of the five permanent members of the Security Council has a veto, the effectiveness of the Council will be impaired. Some argue that France's threat to use its veto saved the Security Council from having to authorize military action in Iraq and thus undermine the UN's credibility by sanctioning a dubious war. But it would have been better for the Security Council to come to a consensus on disarming Iraq, unimpeded by the veto, with military action used only as a final option if inspections proved unworkable. It should be remembered that the US has itself frequently used its veto to block broadly supported resolutions critical of Israeli policies toward the Palestinians. Also, on a 14–1 vote, the US single-handedly blocked the re-election of Boutros Boutros-Ghali as Secretary-General; the US considered him too strong an advocate for strengthening the UN's peace-enforcement ability.

The veto cannot be arbitrarily taken away. In fact, had the US, Russia, the UK, France, and China not received such power, the UN would likely not have come into existence. For at least the last decade, a debate has been carried on about enlarging the membership of the Security Council and "softening" the power of the veto (perhaps by requiring at least three of the permanent members to join in a veto). But in the turbulence of the 1990s and first years of the twenty-first century, the lack of agreement on structural reform of the Security Council persists. All of Asia, a diverse region containing over half of humanity, has but one permanent seat on the Council. Africa and Latin America have none. But streamlining many of the UN procedures that Secretary-General Annan is undertaking is paving the way for possible future changes in the composition of the Council itself.

Meanwhile, caught in the throes of one war after another, the UN valiantly holds up a candle of hope for the world. It continues to try to balance the unilateral tendencies of the US with the multilateral needs of the world community and is determined to advance wide-ranging programs to build a culture of peace and supplant the culture of war.

The UN leadership, embodied so well by Kofi Annan, understands very well the complexity at the root of "the UN problem." The UN cannot force governments to adopt enlightened polices for global survival, but it can enforce decisions taken by the Security Council when the veto-wielding states have agreed not to block such decisions. Although such actions, when they are taken, deal for the most part with stopping the excesses of aggression, they never command positive steps for peace. The most the UN can do is encourage states to adopt the global strategies that states have helped develop. The UN has no stick here, only a carrot.

The UN must be able to hold the trust and voluntary co-operation of the member states. The UN leadership must use consummate diplomacy to keep even a spirit of reasonable harmony among states, who bring their divergent interests every day to UN meetings. And the UN leadership must reach beyond governments to build a constituency for action. Although dependent on governments, the UN today is reaching beyond them. The originator of the components of the culture of peace, the UN must tread softly in pushing for their implementation. "Make haste slowly" might well be the UN's motto, for, the urgencies of the peace agenda notwithstanding, it can operate no other way.

PART III

Changing Our Attitude

7

Religions:
A Reconciliation of Peoples

Since the culture of peace aspires to a global ethic of reconciliation, considering religion as a prime conveyor of the new culture should be natural. History shows that the true shapers of past cultures and civilizations have not been political leaders so much as spiritual leaders: Confucius, Buddha, Abraham, Moses, Jesus, Paul, and Mohammed. Their teachings have shaped values and ethics, informed social systems, and evaluated the justice and injustice of political, economic, and social systems.

Yet what stands out in history are the wars of religion. The wars waged from the thirteenth century through the sixteenth were a militant chapter in the history of the Christian church in the West. Christians persecuted Jews and led crusades against Muslims. They even waged wars against other Christians. These wars were fought in the name of God. They filled many people with horror and distrust of religion. A secularization of the West followed and a new faith in science and technology replaced religion as the shaper of civilization.

Today, many people ask: Can religions resolve conflict or do religions cause conflict?

To answer this question, we must first look at how the essential message of peace at the heart of the great religions of the world has been distorted. The events of September 11, 2001, are a prime example.

Islam: A Compassionate Religion

A few days after the attacks on the World Trade Center and the Pentagon, I was invited to a Muslim prayer service in the Al Rashid mosque in my home city of Edmonton. I joined a number of Christians and Jews to pray for peace alongside our Muslim neighbours. The Imam, Shaban Sheriff, deeply concerned at the backlash against Muslims because the suicide terrorists were young Muslim men, said that Islam stands upon the pillars of justice and peace. He challenged his congregation to show the people of our community that they were good citizens who abhorred violence of any kind. The Imam was chagrined that Osama bin Laden, widely assumed to be the force behind the hijackings in the US, had cited the Koran, Islam's holiest book, as the inspiration for the terrorist attacks.

The more bin Laden revealed himself in subsequent months, the more it became clear that his motivation was not the Koran but his hatred of the secularism of the United States, which he held responsible for the increasing decadence he saw in Muslim countries. Nonetheless, selective quotations from the Koran were used by some in the West to endorse the view that Islam is essentially a fanatical and violent faith. In the months following the terrorist attacks, the number of anti-Muslim hate crimes increased.

Muslim scholars around the world, reacting with revulsion to the terrorist actions, tried to explain that Islam is a peaceful, progressive, inherently forgiving, and com-passionate religion. But Islam, no less than Christianity or Judaism, is subject to extremists who claim that their "war" against oppression is just. Christians have killed in the name of God, as have Hindus, Buddhists, Jews, and others. In the wake of September 11, Muslims, too, have been accused of turning "divine commandments" into a divine license to kill. We must resist this "hijacking" of the Muslim faith.

Islam is the third of the three revealed religions, following Judaism and Christianity. "The religions of Abraham all worship the same God," says Karen Armstrong, an internationally recognized non-Muslim historian of Islam. "All three have a deep commitment to compassion, justice and peace."

The Koran, as revealed to the Prophet Mohammed in the seventh century, is the bearer of the final message and last revelation from God, according to Muslim belief. The root of the word Islam is *silm*, meaning peace—peace with God and man. Islam means surrender to the will of God, and a Muslim is one who submits to God's will. The five obligations of a Muslim are: a declaration and acceptance of the oneness of God and the prophethood of Mohammed; prayer five times a day, if possible in a mosque; charity, generally 2.5 per cent of one's wealth annually; fasting from dawn to dusk for 30 days in the month of Ramadan; and pilgrimage at least once in a lifetime to Mecca to perform the hajj if one is in good health and can afford to do so. Islam is both a religion and a way of life that promotes social harmony and solidarity through its sacred texts as well as its traditional and ethical systems and lived experiences.

In numerous verses, the Koran exhorts believers to refrain from war and violence. Only if threatened with aggression is fighting allowed. The Koran says:

> Allah only forbids you respecting those who made war upon you on account of [your] religion, and drove you forth from your homes and backed up [others] in your expulsion, that you make friends with them, and whoever makes friends with them, these are the unjust. (Koran: 60:9)

And fight in the way of Allah with those who fight with you, and do not exceed the limits, surely Allah does not love those who exceed the limits. (Koran: 2:190)

And if they incline to peace, then incline to it and trust in Allah; surely He is the Hearing, the Knowing. (Koran: 8:61)

The full picture of Islam and the Koran is captured by Chapter 5, Verse 32:

For this reason did We prescribe to the children of Israel that whoever slays a soul, unless it be for manslaughter or for mischief in the land, it is as though he slew all men; and whoever keeps it alive, it is as though he kept alive all men; and certainly Our apostles came to them with clear arguments, but even after that many of them certainly act extravagantly in the land.

Islam does not fully advocate passivity. It permits the use of force when Muslims are not allowed to practise their faith, when people are oppressed and subjugated, and when people's land is forcibly taken from them. But indiscriminate fighting is prohibited; women, children, and innocent civilians are to be protected. The term *jihad*, so often misunderstood in the West, means "exertion on the path toward God." It is a struggle with one's base spirits: sin, oppression, greed, and exploitation. In its deepest sense, it is an inner personal exertion, not a holy war, although it can also become an outer defensive action to protect one's community. The Muslim faith does not countenance a *jihad* against the West: far from it. Muslim communities around the world were horrified that their faith was so abused and made an instrument of evil by terrorist sects. Their martyrdom was not holy, but a wicked perversion.

As Karen Armstrong writes:

It would be as grave a mistake to see Osama bin Laden as an authentic representative of Islam as to consider James Kopp, the alleged killer of an abortion provider in Buffalo,

N.Y., a typical Christian or Baruch Goldstein, who shot 29 worshipers in the Hebron mosque in 1994 and died in the attack, a true martyr of Israel. The vast majority of Muslims, who are horrified by the atrocity of Sept. 11, must reclaim their faith from those who have so violently hijacked it.

Classic Islamic civilization sees itself as the true bridge between West and East. Some scholars hold that what is sometimes viewed as a "clash of civilizations" is really a clash of symbols. The symbols on the one side are head scarves, turbans, and other forms of garb and beard that many Westerners find offensive, just as fundamentalist Muslims view much of Western culture as anti-Islamic. Western arrogance (of which there has been plenty in the colonial era) breeds contempt and fanaticism on the Islamic side. Paranoia exists on both sides. The Islamic world is offended by the West's cultural triumphalism, backed up by overwhelming military force.

The shared cultural roots joining Islam and the West, too often forgotten, were swept aside in the fearful period following September 11. To counteract this, many conferences have been held to affirm the central point that Islam does not teach Muslims to kill innocent people in the name of a political agenda. A group of American writers contributed to a book, *Taking Back Islam*, which attempted to "reclaim their faith" first of all from Muslim extremists but also from a leadership that many contributors find still rooted, physically or psychologically, in other lands and other cultures. In her contribution to the book, Karen Armstrong recounts how Mohammed was shocked to learn of the theological differences between Jews and Christians. "It seemed perverse and wrong to him that people who surrendered their entire lives to God should quarrel with one another about abstruse theological matters – it was God that mattered, not how people interpreted their experience of the divine." Mohammed believed that Jews, Muslims, and

Christians should stress the things that unite them instead of exalting their own traditions at the expense of other faiths. Armstrong writes:

> We need to cultivate this "Abrahamic" spirit during these terrible days. All of us – Jews, Christians, and Muslims – have used our religions to denigrate and even to persecute others. But Abraham is our common father, and if we can use September 11 to realize that we must not exalt our own faiths at the expense of others', perhaps something good can come out of evil.

> If the atrocity is used by Christians and Jews to ostracize all Muslims and to denounce their faith as inherently evil, then it would not simply be Islam that was in danger of being hijacked on September 11, but Judaism and Christianity too.

The Fundamentalist Opposition

All religious communities bear a great responsibility today to demonstrate that their values, standards, and attitudes can ameliorate conflict and create the conditions for peace. Religions need to answer the charge that they are the root cause of the hatred and fanaticism that motivated the terrorist attacks. It is not just Islam and Judaism that need to respond. The killings inflicted by Catholics and Protestants in Northern Ireland are a sad example of internecine strife within Christianity. The religious voice, while not silent, is muted or blurred considering the level of hatred and animosity persistent around the world. Religion seems to be constrained by the fundamentalist elements within it that prevent it from speaking with one voice to the wounds of conflict.

In *The Battle for God*, Karen Armstrong describes the fundamentalism that has emerged in every major religious tradition as an impediment to religious co-operation for

the common good. Fundamentalists are generally characterized as those spiritually engaged in a conflict with enemies
whose secularist policies and beliefs seem inimical to religion
itself. Fundamentalists experience this as a cosmic war
between the forces of good and evil. They fear annihilation
and try to fortify themselves with a selective retrieval of
certain doctrines and practices of the past. Usually guided
by charismatic leaders, they refine their religious
"fundamentals" so as to create an ideology that provides the
faithful with a plan of action. Fundamentalists pit themselves
against the secularism that drives so many societies today. In
doing so, they neglect the more tolerant, inclusive, and
compassionate teachings of religion and cultivate theologies
of rage, resentment, and revenge. They also attempt to make
a secular world sacred again. Christian fundamentalists, for
example, reject the discoveries of biology and physics about
the origins of life. Jewish fundamentalists observe their
revealed law more stringently than ever before. Muslim and
Jewish fundamentalists both interpret the Arab-Israeli
conflict, which began as a secular conflict, in an exclusively
religious way. Armstrong writes:

> It is only a small minority of fundamentalists who commit
> acts of terror, but even the most peaceful and law-abiding
> are perplexing, because they seem so adamantly opposed
> to many of the most positive values of modern society.
> Fundamentalists have no time for democracy, pluralism,
> religious toleration, peacekeeping, free speech, or the
> separation of church and state.

On occasion, a small minority pervert religion to
sanction murder. Fundamentalist ideologies are rooted in
fear. Armstrong says that the desire to define doctrines, erect
barriers, establish borders, and separate the faithful in a sacred
enclave where the law is stringently observed springs from
a terror of extinction. This terror has made all fundamentalists,
at one time or another, believe that the secularists were about
to wipe them out. "The modern world, which seems so

exciting to a liberal, seems Godless," says Armstrong, "drained of meaning, and even satanic to a fundamentalist."

It is true that the modern, secularist world seems to have little time for God, except as a sort of pageantry. The best of religion, however, does not set itself up as a fortress but rather seeks to infuse society with love and compassion, not hostility and revenge. Religions are so caught up in mediating among their own members that their potential is diffused. It is a great loss to the world that the moderates, that is, the great majority, within religions are inhibited from extending their spiritual values to the public on a daily basis. The culture of peace needs the examples of peace and reconciliation in keeping with the sacred texts and teachings of religious communities.

The abuse or misuse of religion has undoubtedly darkened the pages of history of places like Northern Ireland and the Balkans. But, as the former Archbishop of Canterbury, Dr. George Carey, reminds us: those who condemn religion for its alleged destructive power in world affairs should remember that the evils perpetrated by the messianic regimes of Stalin, Hitler, and Pol Pot "were the result of those who eschewed religion."

Adherents of the world's religions should not lose confidence that they can help to resolve conflict. Faith communities help to shape societies and cultures through the core values they proclaim. Interfaith co-operation can make shared values more evident. Religious leaders can contribute to conciliation and mediate efforts. In addition to the charismatic leadership of such people as Mahatma Gandhi, Martin Luther King, and Desmond Tutu, one thinks of Bishop Carlos Belo in East Timor, whose vision, courage, and remarkable spiritual leadership is universally admired and was recognized with the Nobel Peace Prize. Also, faith communities can give voice to the marginalized and poor. While the roots of conflict are deep and tangled, many of them are embedded in the soil of poverty, ignorance, and debt. These problems ought to be a basic concern for religion, which can speak with one voice on behalf of the poor of the earth.

A Core Teaching of All

All the major religions teach the essence of the culture of peace: Do not do unto others what you do not want done to you. This Golden Rule, or the ethic of reciprocity, is found in the scriptures of nearly every religion and is often regarded as the most concise and general principle of ethics.

I do not mean to suggest that there are not important differences between religions. There are. We live in a world of differences. But differences must not be allowed to obscure our much more significant commonalities. These commonalities centre on the oneness of the human family. We all need fresh air, food, water, shelter, and the opportunity to develop ourselves. These human rights are inherent in our human nature. Religion ought to help us affirm these commonalities in an equitable and just manner. Religion should not be misused as an instrument for division and injustice, betraying the very ideals and teachings that lie at the heart of each of the world's great traditions. Religion must find a way for its spiritual traditions to have their diverse communities work in harmony for the common good. Religious communities are the largest and best-organized civil institutions in the world today, claiming the allegiance of billions of believers. They are uniquely equipped to meet modern challenges: resolving conflicts, caring for the sick and needy, and promoting peaceful co-existence among all peoples.

The Golden Rule

Bahá'í Faith

And if thine eyes be turned towards justice, choose thou for thy neighbour that which thou choosest for thyself.
Epistle to the Son of the Wolf, 30

Hindu Faith

This is the sum of duty: do naught to others which if done to thee would cause thee pain.
The Mahabharata

Jewish Faith

What is hateful to you, do not to your fellow men. That is the entire Law; all the rest is commentary.
The Talmud

Zoroastrian Faith

Whatever is disagreeable to yourself do not do unto others.
Shayast-na-Shayast 13:29

Buddhist Faith

Hurt not others with that which pains yourself.
Udana-Varga

Christian Faith

In everything, do to others as you would have them do to you; for this is the law and the prophets.
The Gospel of Matthew 7:12, The Gospel of Luke 6:31

Muslim Faith

No one of you is a believer until he desires for his brother that which he desires for himself.
Hadith

It is not just a matter of it being proper for religions to infuse values into civilization. The fractures of the modern world brought about by the culture of war make it imperative that religions now rise above denominationalism and, with the full force of the teaching of love and reciprocity that underscores all religions, speak out to build the conditions for peace. Religion cannot become the state. But religion must inspire the state. It must do this not through triumphalism, but through humility—acknowledging its responsibility for many conflicts of the past and expressing its determination now to play a role in achieving peace and social justice.

The first step in playing this role is for religions to come together, not to submerge their identities but to affirm the meaning of life at a time when humanity has acquired the power of total extinction. This role must go beyond mere admonitions of tolerance. The goal must be much more than overcoming religious prejudice. The crisis of our time requires religions to speak to the consciences of humanity with a message of unity. We have one destiny. We live or die together in the struggle for peace. All humanity—with its differences of race, religion, and culture—must recognize the common danger to life and use this crisis to ascend to a higher level of civilization. This goal requires nothing less for humanity to mature.

Parliament of the World's Religions

The struggle to find a global ethic that all religions can support can be dated back to 1893, when representatives of Eastern and Western spiritual traditions convened a Parliament of the World's Religions. Its mission was to cultivate harmony between the world's religious and spiritual communities. Held in Chicago in conjunction with the Columbian Exposition, the Parliament planted the seeds for a worldwide interreligious dialogue. It took nearly a century for the seeds to produce some flowers. When the centenary of the Parliament occurred in 1993, 200 scholars and theologians signed on to a "Declaration of the Religions for a Global Ethic."

This was solemnly proclaimed at the World Parliament of Religions, again held in Chicago and attended by 6,500 persons. The chief author of the text was Hans Küng, one of the key theologians at the Second Vatican Council, whose writings have acted as a catalyst in interfaith work for many years. Küng has said there will be no survival without a world ethic, no world peace without peace between the religions, and no peace between the religions without dialogue between the religions.

The preamble of the Declaration is a trenchant call to action by the world's religions because "the world is in agony." Küng insisted that the Declaration not focus on the juridical or political levels, but rather on the ethical level: "the level of binding values, irrevocable standards, and interior fundamental attitudes." The Declaration had to be capable of producing a consensus. Hence, disputed moral questions (such as abortion or euthanasia) were excluded. "Our different religions and cultural traditions must not prevent our common involvement in opposing all forms of inhumanity and working for greater humanness."

The heart of the Declaration is the expression of a "global ethic." History has shown that

- A better global order cannot be created or enforced by laws, prescriptions, and conventions alone.

- The realization of peace, justice, and the protection of Earth depends on the insight and readiness of men and women to act justly;

- Action in favour of rights and freedoms presumes a consciousness of responsibility and duty, and that therefore both the minds and hearts of women and men must be addressed;

- Rights without morality cannot long endure, and that there will be no better global order without a global ethic.

The Preamble of the Declaration of a Global Ethic

The world is in agony. The agony is so pervasive and urgent that we are compelled to name its manifestations so that the depth of this pain may be made clear.

Peace eludes us…the planet is being destroyed…neighbors live in fear…women and men are estranged from each other…children die!

This is abhorrent!

We condemn the abuses of Earth's ecosystems.

We condemn the poverty that stifles life's potential; the hunger that weakens the human body; the economic disparities that threaten so many families with ruin.

We condemn the social disarray of the nations; the disregard for justice which pushes citizens to the margin; the anarchy overtaking our communities; and the insane death of children from violence. In particular we condemn aggression and hatred in the name of religion.

But this agony need not be.

It need not be because the basis for an ethic already exists. This ethic offers the possibility of a better individual and global order, and leads individuals away from despair and societies away from chaos.

We are women and men who have embraced the precepts and practices of the world's religions:

We affirm that a common set of core values is found in the teachings of the religions, and that these form the basis of a global ethic.

We affirm that this truth is already known, but yet to be lived in heart and action.

We affirm that there is an irrevocable, unconditional norm for all areas of life, for families and communities, for races, nations, and religions. There already exist ancient guidelines for human behavior which are found in the teachings of the religions of the world and which are the condition for a sustainable world order.

By a global ethic, I do not mean a global ideology or a single unified religion beyond all existing religions, and certainly not the domination of one religion over all others. By a global ethic, I mean a fundamental consensus of binding values, irrevocable standards, and personal attitudes. Without such a fundamental consensus on an ethic, sooner or later every community will be threatened by chaos or dictatorship, and individuals will despair.

Religions cannot solve the economic, environmental, political, and social problems of the Earth. But they can provide "a change in the inner orientation" so that the political systems will be pressed to treat every human being humanely. The Golden Rule was cited and put in positive terms: "What you wish done to yourself, do to others!"

Here in summary are the four "irrevocable directives" that Küng presents:

Toward a Culture of Non-Violence and Respect for Life

No one has the right to physically or psychologically torture, injure, much less kill, any other human being. And no people, no state, no race, or no religion have the right to hate, to discriminate, to "cleanse," to exile, much less to liquidate a "foreign" minority that is different in behaviour or holds different beliefs. Persons who hold political power must work within the framework of a just order and commit themselves to the most non-violent, peaceful solutions possible. Every people, every race, and every religion must show tolerance and respect—indeed high appreciation—for every other.

Toward a Culture of Solidarity and a Just Economic Order

Where extreme poverty reigns, helplessness and despair spread. Where power and wealth are accumulated ruthlessly, feelings of envy, resentment, deadly hatred, and rebellion inevitably well up in the disadvantaged and marginalized.

This leads to a vicious circle of violence and counter-violence. Let no one be deceived: there is no global peace without global justice. We must utilize economic and political power for service to humanity instead of misusing it in ruthless battles for domination. We must develop a spirit of compassion with those who suffer, with special care for children, the aged, the poor, the disabled, refugees, and the lonely.

Toward a Culture of Tolerance and a Life of Truthfulness

Despite the numerous persons who strive to lead lives of honesty and truthfulness, all over the world we find endless lies and deceit, swindling, hypocrisy, ideology, and demagoguery. The ancient religions and ethical traditions command us to speak and act truthfully. The media today are duty bound to objectivity, fairness, and the preservation of human dignity; they have no right to manipulate public opinion or distort reality. Political leaders, when they lie in the faces of their people, forsake their credibility and deserve to lose their offices. Those acting in the name of religion who stir up prejudice, hatred, and enmity toward those of different beliefs deserve condemnation.

Toward a Culture of Equal Rights and Partnership Between Men and Women

Sexual exploitation and sexual discrimination are condemned for being degrading to all humanity. We have the duty to resist wherever the domination of one sex over the other is preached—even in the name of religious conviction; wherever sexual exploitation is tolerated; and where prostitution is fostered or children abused. The relationship between women and men should be characterized not by patronizing behaviour or exploitation, but by love, partnership, and trustworthiness. The social institution of marriage should guarantee security and mutual support to husband, wife, and child. It should secure the rights of all family members.

Is such a global ethic attainable? Of course it is. The World Parliament of Religions, showing a sense of optimism, continues to focus on the conditions for peace, sustainable development, and ways to protect and promote respect for cultural diversity. Religions are instrumentally placed to effect a transformation in the consciousness of individuals and in public life. But religions first have to rise above their internal preoccupations and reach out to humanity. Such a reaching out occurred during the Second Vatican Council when the Council Fathers adopted the Pastoral Constitution on the Church in the Modern World. The opening words resonate with the intentions of the World Parliament. The Council said:

> The joys and hopes, the griefs and anxieties of the [people] of this age, especially those who are poor or in any way afflicted, these too are the joys and hopes, the griefs and anxieties of the followers of Christ. Indeed, nothing genuinely human fails to raise an echo in their hearts.

The Council went on to say that the equal dignity of all persons demands that a more humane and just condition of life be brought about. It said that excessive economic and social differences between the members of the one human family militate against social justice, equity, the dignity of the human person, as well as social and international peace. The World Council of Churches, a fellowship of 342 churches in 120 countries, has published similar statements of concern for all of humanity, notably a study document stimulating reflection and action to overcome violence.

World Conference on Religion and Peace

Interfaith activities are difficult to sustain. A recurring fear is that the unique characteristics of a particular tradition will be lost within the larger group. The 1950s and 1960s saw a growth in interfaith initiatives, especially in the years following the Second Vatican Council. In 1970, a group of religious leaders brought together in Kyoto an assembly of the major faiths: Baha'i, Buddhist, Christian, Confucian, Hindu, Jain, Jewish, Muslim, Shinto, Sikh, and Zoroastrian. The group became the World Conference on Religion and Peace (WCRP), an historic attempt to convene men and women of all major religions on a regular basis to discuss urgent issues of peace. The group found they shared these common beliefs:

- A conviction of the fundamental unity of the human family, and the equality and dignity of all human beings

- A sense of the sacredness of the individual person and his or her conscience

- A sense of the value of the human community

- A realization that might is not right; that human power is not self-sufficient and absolute

- A belief that love, compassion, selflessness, and the force of inner truthfulness and of the spirit have ultimately greater power than hate, enmity, and self-interest

- A sense of obligation to stand on the side of the poor and the oppressed as against oppressors

- A profound hope that good will finally prevail.

WCRP endured, though it cannot be said that the official structures of the religions it embraced were particularly helpful. The new organization, which works closely with the non-governmental organization (NGO) community attached to the UN, has become the largest international coalition of representatives from the world's great religions who are dedicated to achieving peace. Dr. William Vendley, WCRP Secretary-General, says: "Today as people around the world appear to be captured by old hatreds and seized by deadly conflicts, the importance of mobilizing the peacemaking and co-operative possibilities of the world's religious communities has perhaps never been greater."

Respecting cultural differences while celebrating their common humanity, WCRP is active on every continent and in some of the most troubled places on earth, creating multi-religious partnerships. Some of WCRP's successes include mediating dialogue among warring factions in Sierra Leone, building a new climate of reconciliation in Bosnia and Kosovo, organizing an international network of religious women's organizations, and launching a program to assist the millions of children affected by the HIV/AIDS pandemic in Africa. WCRP holds world assemblies every five years. At the most recent—in Amman, Jordan, in 1999—the assembly brought together delegates and participants from 15 religious traditions and from 70 countries.

The Amman assembly resulted in a statement stressing the importance for religions to foster a culture of peace: "The diversity of cultures and traditions can be affirmed and celebrated, just as the commonalities are also recognized, shared and celebrated." Religious leadership in the movement for peace must begin with the reconciliation of the religious institutions themselves. "True reconciliation requires the painful acknowledgement that both religious patterns and the actions of religiously motivated people have also caused conflict, suffering and pain. ... Reconciliation requires the search for truth and the acknowledgement of accountability, processes that can be liberating." The Amman statement added that the transmission of values into the third millennium must include a broader understanding and respect for the values and contributions of diverse religions and cultures. In this way, a shared culture of peace may be the beneficiary of not just one tradition but of the rich legacy of diverse heritages.

> The one place where all peoples presently come together is the United Nations. Its charter mandates the achievement of peace, the fulfillment of human rights, the institution of the rule of law, and the promotion of better standards of life for all people. One finds at the

United Nations, symbolic testimony to our spiritual commitments. It is found in the artistic and cultural artifacts that are visible in its corridors. The world can read there the words that we are to beat our swords into ploughshares, our spears into pruning hooks; that we are to do unto others what we would have others do unto us; and that we have been made of a common humanity and that the most honoured among us are the most righteous.

Moving Beyond Religion

In our secular society, such religious affirmations are compartmentalized. The media—and hence the political establishment, for the most part—treat the social justice teaching of the churches as a special interest. Many in public life think that something advocated by a religious group is automatically suspect. The separation of church and state is so deep that only secularism is trusted. It is as though religious values and the public good live on two different planets.

Religions and their adherents are indeed paying a heavy price for their excesses of the past. They must, however, become emboldened to present the framework for a new global ethic to modern society in the sure knowledge that secularism, for all of its technological prowess, has robbed the human soul of meaning. The modern crisis of humanity has come about because secularism has driven public policies, which have bowed to the claims of the rich over the needs of the poor. But waging a war against secularism is not the answer. Rather, what the world urgently needs is sharing and communicating the insights into the human condition from as many different perspectives and traditions as possible.

In playing this role, religion must go beyond religion. The World Parliament of Religions closed its Declaration with an invitation to all men and women—"*whether religious or not*"—to join in a common global ethic. In other words, the values that underlie the common teaching of the religions must—to be heard in secular society—be communicated in non-religious language.

That these values do indeed exist in secular society was reflected by the Commission on Global Governance, a group of 28 international public figures headed by Ingvar Carlsson, former Prime Minister of Sweden, and Shridath Ramphal, former Secretary-General of the Commonwealth. The Commission, presenting proposals for improving the world's governance and better managing its affairs, published its report, *Our Global Neighbourhood*, in 1995. Remarkably, this secular, multicultural Commission devoted the second chapter to a discussion of the values needed to give stability to societies. These values relate to the sanctity of life, "a concept shared by people of all faiths as well as by secular humanists." As the report continues:

> We believe that all humanity could uphold the core values of respect for life, liberty, justice and equity, mutual respect, caring, and integrity. These provide a foundation for transforming a global neighbourhood based on economic exchange and improved communications into a universal moral community in which people are bound together by more than proximity, interest, or identity. They all derive in one way or another from the principle, which is in accord with religious teachings around the world, that people should treat others as they would themselves wish to be treated. It is this imperative that was reflected in the call made in the UN Charter for recognition of "the inherent dignity and equal and inalienable rights of all members of the human family".

In the words of the Commission, a shared sense of values can help people see beyond immediate clashes of interest and act on behalf of a larger, long-term, and mutual interest. Chief among these values is a respect for life and its corollary, non-violence. Human beings are born equal in their right to human dignity and are entitled to certain basic liberties: to define and express their own identity, to choose their form of worship, to earn a livelihood, to be free from persecution and oppression, and to receive information. Basic liberties also include free speech, a free press, and the right to vote. Without these, the world becomes a battleground of warring individuals, factions, and groups, with each seeking to protect its particular interests or to impose its authority on others.

The Commission also recognized justice and equity as essential human values. Although people are born into wildly unequal economic and social circumstances, such disparities in their conditions or life chances affront our human sense of justice. Tolerance is also indispensable for peaceful relations in any society. The world community must become resolute in upholding respect for other people, other races, other beliefs, other sexual orientations, and other cultures.

Further, the Commission noted, the quality of life in any society depends to a great extent on the degree to which its members accept a duty to care for their neighbours. The instincts of caring and compassion provide the impulse for humanitarian action—and for sharing with those less advantaged—that all societies need. Also, integrity is the basis of trust that is necessary in relationships among people and organizations.

Like the World Parliament of Religions, the Commission called for a global ethic that should "seek to ensure that international society is imbued by a civic spirit." Here, all citizens—not just governments—should accept the obligation to recognize and help protect the rights of others. And rights need to be joined with responsibilities, since rights can only be preserved if they are exercised responsibly and with due respect for the reciprocal rights of others.

We therefore urge the international community to unite in support of a global ethic of common rights and shared responsibilities. In our view, such an ethic—reinforcing the fundamental rights that are already part of the fabric of international norms—would provide the moral foundation for constructing a more effective system of global governance.

The Commission listed the rights and responsibilities that constitute the minimum basis for defining a more civil global society. It expressed the hope that these principles could some day be embodied in a binding international document—a Global Charter of Civil Society. Such a Charter would encompass the rights of all people to

- a secure life

- equitable treatment

- an opportunity to earn a fair living and provide for their own welfare

- the definition and preservation of their differences through peaceful means

- participation in governance at all levels

- free and fair petition for redress of gross injustices

- equal access to information

- equal access to the global commons.

At the same time as exercising these rights, all people share a responsibility to

- contribute to the common good

- consider the impact of their actions on the security and welfare of others

- promote equity, including gender equity

- protect the interests of future generations by pursuing sustainable development and safeguarding the global commons

- preserve humanity's cultural and intellectual heritage

- be active participants in governance

- work to eliminate corruption.

The global ethic of counterbalanced rights and responsibilities, called for by the Commission on Global Governance, is not expressed in religious language. Yet the prescriptions posed in this language are wholly consonant with the core teaching of the major religions. The agenda for human security contained in the work of the UN Commissions of the 1990s—of which the Commission on Global Governance is but one offshoot—is an expression of moral concern for the well-being of all humanity. The religions of the world should subscribe to it enthusiastically and they should also become fully involved in supporting and promoting the Millennium Goals. What religions have been teaching throughout their histories, secular society is now trying to implement. In this case, at least, religion and society want the same thing.

Bridging the Chasm with Secularism

Some will say that this is an agenda of secular humanism and is devoid of the linkage between humankind and God: namely, that we must love our brothers and sisters who are all made in God's likeness, and our love for them must reflect our love for God. Religion thus restrains its co-operation with secularism, because secularism does not overtly pay its respect to religion as the messenger of God's love. Since secularism is wary of religion (when not downright hostile), religion keeps its distance from secularism. This chasm deprives society of benefiting from the combined influence of secular humanists and religion. It is time for this stand-offishness by both sides to end.

Today, religious leadership, in a spirit of humility and service, should take the first step and, with a united voice, loudly proclaim support for the UN global strategies of disarmament, development, equity, and justice—these elements are the basis for the culture of peace. Religions and their adherents should remember that here on Earth we have the responsibility to continue and protect God's plan of creation. The preservation of the planet must be assured as a first step in the expression of our love for God. Religions will not lose by joining enthusiastically with secular humanists in the promotion of a global ethic that centres on the well-being of humanity. On the contrary, religions will thus manifest their deep concern for the application of the social justice principles embodied in the Golden Rule. Religions will then truly be in the service of God.

It does not seem to me that a global ethic to solidify the culture of peace can be achieved by either secular humanists or religious followers talking only among themselves. It will take an enormous push by the combined forces of civil society, a point to which I return in Chapter 9. Here, I want to underline the prime duty of religions to work alongside the representatives of politics, business, and the financial world to foster the recognition that a global ethic is necessary for the survival of the planet. Hans Küng has said that it has become increasingly clear to him in recent years that the one world in which we live has a chance for survival only if there is no longer any room in it for spheres of differing, contradictory, and even antagonistic ethics. "This one world needs one basic ethic. This one world society certainly does not need a unitary religion and a unitary ideology, but it does need some norms, values, ideals and goals to bring it together and to be binding on it," writes Küng.

Like Küng, although I have a home in my own church, I feel responsible toward all churches and religions: the unity of the churches and peace among all religions. The credibility of religion increasingly depends on putting more stress on what unites followers and less on what divides us. Dialogue—genuine, respectful conversations motivated by a common desire to serve humanity—is now critical.

Hans Küng was a chief contributor to the UN's Dialogue Among Civilizations, which produced the book *Crossing the Divide*, to which I have already referred. The book makes the point that humanity has shared a set of common values over centuries; those who communicate across the cultural divides are more likely to see diversity as a strength and celebrate it as a gift.

The participants in this unique exercise said that reconciliation is the highest form of dialogue. It includes the capacity to listen, the capacity not only to convince but also to be convinced, and, most of all, the capacity to extend forgiveness. Reconciliation cannot be dealt with only at the institutional level; it is a challenge to the hearts and minds of individuals. Reconciliation demands that we seek peace with ourselves first. Reconciliation after warfare is a colossal undertaking. Do our institutions have the capacity to appeal to the heart and soul of those who have to take the first step toward reconciliation? Denial of reconciliation may lead us unconsciously into a perpetual state of hatred, if not a perpetual state of war. Reconciliation is dangerous; charismatic leaders have been assassinated because they tried to cross the divide. Nonetheless, reconciliation, and the refusal to believe that vengeance is justice may well be the cutting edge of a social ethic yet to come. The greatest courage is not to kill the one who stands across the divide, but to look for another way, one that perhaps we have never tried before. The so-called courage of might clearly may hide a weakness of mind, and we must look for new leaders who are unafraid to be in the vanguard of reconciliation. Reconciliation is not for the weak of heart, but rather for those who are prepared to search for it. Reconciliation, Dialogue participants suggest, is the route toward establishing a global ethic.

> A global ethic for institutions and civil society, for leaders and for followers, requires a longing and striving for peace, longing and striving for justice, longing and striving for partnerships, longing and striving for truth. These might be the four pillars of a system of a global ethic that reconciliation, as the new answer to the vicious circle of endless hatred, is going to provide us.

Pope John Paul II reinforced the transformative power of reconciliation, fully understood, when he made an appeal for justice and forgiveness in his 2002 World Day of Peace address:

> No peace without justice, no justice without forgiveness: this is what I wish to say to those responsible for the future of the human community...

Those who dismiss the work of the Dialogue as either irrelevant or a luxury or a form of appeasement should think again, especially following the attacks of September 11. The vulnerability of everyone to murder because each is "different" from the murderer means we must find ways to apply justice in a non-violent manner. The Dialogue among Civilizations sends a signal that diversity is not a threat: it is an essential wealth the world society has yet to fully discover. The terrorists, the irresponsible politicians, and the bigots may well be active and vociferous, but they certainly are a minority. They are prominent because their strong suit is destruction, which takes little time and marginal courage. To build, to discover, and to strive for achievements that will benefit all human beings takes more courage, more effort, and more time. "Whether we are moving towards a clash of civilizations, or towards greater human solidarity against those who murder innocents only because they are different, is really up to each of us." We have two options. We can let the small minority take over and throw us into continuous conflict at all levels. Or we can enlarge the coalition of those who respect each other's dignity and common humanity, and who value the lives of our family members as well as the lives of our fellow human beings on the other side of the planet.

Religions ought to be at the head of the line of those who advocate the ethical responsibility of individuals to expand their circle of concern to encompass people of other nations. The oneness of humanity—long understood by religions—has moved from being a kind of abstract, if vaguely interesting, idea to an issue of pressing daily political concern. The interdependence of world systems now poses unprecedented challenges to national governments. Whether in the area of crime, health, the environment, or the fight against terrorism, interdependence, as Kofi Annan has noted, "has become a reality in our own lives."

Numerous efforts, secularly based, are now underway to establish ethical modes of conduct. The Earth Charter, a "people's document" prepared by a coalition of NGOs, presents a set of ethics and principles to guide humanity toward ways of living that do not deplete the Earth's resources and damage its ability to sustain life. Mary Robinson, former President of Ireland and former UN High Commissioner for Human Rights, has begun the "Ethical Globalization Initiative." This is an effort to bridge existing ideological barriers between different perspectives on human rights and to integrate these rights into economic and social policies affecting globalization. The phenomenon of globalization, so much talked about today, cries out for the application of ethical norms.

If religions do not become more prominently associated with this twenty-first-century struggle of humanity to find ways to live together in one world, then religions will find themselves even more marginalized from the decision-making processes. Religions must change their present attitude of waiting for the world to come to them. Religions must enter—perhaps re-enter—the modern world in a humble and co-operative mode. They must now reach out to make loving contact and help to heal a suffering humanity.

8

Education:
A "Weapon" for Peace

Peace is a wonderful word with a sublime meaning, yet our society as a whole is afraid to embrace it, to nourish it, to celebrate it, and to rejoice in the wholeness of our humanity that peace represents. Every year, the public pays tribute to fallen warriors of past conflicts. From time to time, some march against the idea of a new war. But we do not inculcate into our daily lives the very essence of peace so that it is constantly reflected in all the pageantry and policies of society. Although we honour the winners of the Nobel Peace Prize, we shun the idea of making peace education compulsory for all children.

Advocates of the culture of peace hope to change this so that the operational norms of modern life become a respect for all life, rejection of violence, sharing with others, preservation of the planet, and acceptance of the common ground we all live on. The best, if not the only, way to bring this about is through education.

For too long, the business of conflict resolution and peacebuilding has been left to the experts and assumed to be too technical for the average citizen, let alone the world's youth. However, today's security dilemmas are too multifaceted to be left in the hands of an elite few. To make the transition to a culture of peace, we need to educate each other and ourselves about the technicalities that have been allowed to obscure the fundamental security issues. People at all levels need to be empowered to assess and evaluate the possibilities for change.

Peace education can help humanity move beyond the kind of calamity that has engulfed past and current generations. It is a necessary investment in future generations. It helps to activate our human potential, free from outside interference. Yet it requires a massive effort to better shape our children's consciousness by presenting them with values of tolerance and respect for cultural, religious, and political diversity. This is a challenge so broad that it must become the sustained priority at all levels of life. This can be accomplished, but only if governments, communities, and individuals take the culture of peace to heart and mind.

Peace education certainly belongs inside the traditional education system—from nursery school to post-doctoral programs. Although formal education is crucial, people learn at every stage of life. This is why I suggest we should take advantage of every opportunity to transmit knowledge about the key peace education themes of co-operation, conflict resolution, non-violence, human rights, social justice, world resources, global environment, and multicultural under-standing. The media, the Internet, the work of non-governmental organizations (NGOs), and participation in community life all provide ways in which we learn about the world around us. I think also of the millions upon millions of children in developing countries who receive no, or minimal, education as a result of the misplaced spending priorities of governments. I think of the ignorance, bigotry, and intolerance communicated all around us that shore up the culture of war. Education, then, is a very big subject that goes far beyond the classroom.

New Teaching Encounters

There is a pressing need to combat ignorance, complacency, and the culture of violence. We need to recognize that peace education—in a world that has been careening directionless in the post-Cold War years—is more necessary than ever before to develop a planetary consciousness. We must put peace education in a broad framework. The definition I favour is this:

> ... teaching encounters that draw out from people their desires for peace and provide them with nonviolent alternatives for managing conflicts, as well as the skills for critical analysis of the structural arrangements that legitimate and produce injustice and inequality.

This definition is provided by Professor Ian Harris, Executive Director of the Peace Education Commission and of the International Peace Research Association, and John Synott, a peace educator based at the Queensland University of Technology. It treats peace education not only as a subject in its own right, which it certainly is, but also as a perspective. It helps us to examine critically the major issues affecting humanity and to participate actively in society around us. Most importantly, it helps us to foster certain attitudes that the new generation especially needs to cope with the increasing complexity of life. Some of the attitudes evoked by peace education include:

- Curiosity, both intellectual and cultural

- Appreciation of diversity, receptivity to new perspectives, and a sense of commonality of humankind's needs, rights, aspirations, and talents

- Concern for justice, commitment to equality

- Tolerance of uncertainty, conflict, and change

- Capacity for creativity, risk taking, and thinking in images and symbols

- World awareness, holistic thinking, and a respect for life forms and their place in the web of life.

An attitude of openness helps us to grasp the connections between peace, comprehensive security, and sustainable development in an increasingly interdependent world. It helps us to see linkages so that, for example, we think about the needs of peace in ways that go far beyond the reduction of weaponry. A UN Study on Disarmament and Non-Proliferation Education, published in 2002 by a group of experts after a two-year review, laid out a set of objectives in fostering integrated thinking:

- To learn *how* to think rather than *what* to think about issues

- To develop critical thinking skills in an informed citizenry

- To deepen understanding of the multiple factors at the local, national, regional and global levels that either foster or undermine peace

- To encourage attitudes and actions which promote peace

- To convey relevant information and foster a responsive attitude to current and future security challenges through the development and widespread availability of improved methodologies and research techniques

- To bridge political, regional and technological divides by bringing together ideas, concepts, people, groups and institutions

- To project at all levels the values of peace, tolerance, non-violence, dialogue and consultation as the basis for interaction among peoples, countries and civilizations.

Programming for Peace

Just as minds can be programmed for violence and prejudice, they can also be opened up to the importance of peace and tolerance. To date, education systems have been very successful at increasing literacy and technical skills and thus modernizing national economies. With economic success measured by the number of university degrees per capita and with education ranked alongside corporate tax policy and other economic indicators, education policy is considered as just another factor in determining competitive advantage for those Western countries at the forefront of globalization. But this approach has done little to widen the prospects for peace or sustainable development. Instead, it serves to harden national feeling and competitive individualism. Consequently, the present generation has been left ill-prepared to adapt peaceably to a globalized world demanding precisely the opposite qualities. This is why Pope John Paul II, speaking in 2003 to a congress of university students from 30 countries, emphasized the need to educate future generations in "true peace." He cited the four pillars of peace mentioned by Pope John XXIII in his encyclical *Pacem in Terris*: "truth, justice, love, liberty."

The reality of globalization demands that the current generation, and those who come after, acquire more knowledge and understanding of the world than their elders ever possessed. In a world where our fate is held in common, simply learning to manage conflict within the current war system—through arms control, peacekeeping, and humanitarian assistance, to name a few examples—is not enough. We must do something more profound.

The first step is enabling the coming generation to understand that, in a globalized world, security cannot come from the barrel of a gun. Although threats to security exist at the global scale, our answers and solutions are anchored in an old nation-state system that finds it increasingly difficult to predict or respond to the new security environment. A security defined in terms of human and ecological needs must replace the prevailing definition based on armaments, violent conflict, and war. Adjusting to the new security reality will not be easy, since the strategic interests of the major powers—fed by the military-industrial and scientific complexes—are still the driving forces in international relations.

Peace education offers a concrete strategy that goes beyond the current management approach to violent conflict. More than simply advocating against war, it seeks to create something more systemic and lasting from the bottom up. The foundation of peacebuilding, peace education, goes beyond the science of conflict that preoccupies current curricula. It aims to create the knowledge, skills, and attitudes that will allow people at all ages and levels to develop the behavioural changes needed to prevent the occurrence of violent conflict, resolve it peacefully, and create the social conditions conducive to peace. Certainly, many actions can be taken to make a more humane society in the aftermath of war: disarming combatants, collecting and destroying weapons, repatriating refugees, training security personnel, monitoring elections, and reforming and strengthening governmental institutions. But to cement peace in place, a much deeper and sustained effort is needed to educate present and future generations to use non-violent means to resolve conflict.

The UN is at the cutting edge of this effort. The first special session of the General Assembly on disarmament in 1978 initiated several long-term educational efforts, such as the UN Institute for Disarmament Research. The UN Disarmament Fellowship Programme has trained more than 600 junior diplomats in the details of disarmament negotiations. The UN Study on Disarmament and Non-Proliferation Education provides measures for opening up current curricula to address the complexity of international conflict issues. Specifically, the study recognizes the crucial link between disarmament and other international issues and seeks to raise the level of public engagement through education. It recommends close collaboration between experts in the field and civil society—especially educators and academic institutions. Through education and training, individuals can become empowered to make a contribution to achieving concrete disarmament and non-proliferation measures. The study realizes that the knowledge required by a school-age child in a refugee camp will be different from that needed by a diplomat, but it reflects the key idea that the most effective way to inspire activism, and thus change, is through learning at every stage of life.

Claiming a Priority

It is an irony that, just at the time when the culture of peace is opening up new vistas of thinking, peace studies programs have such a hard time claiming a priority in university budgets. University administrators are pressed to turn out students who can compete in the marketplace, not necessarily question its underlying values. The "commodification of education" stifles alternatives to the status quo. Defence and strategic studies courses, which uphold the status quo, are well established and generously funded. Peace education, though opening up new possibilities for stronger economies everywhere, goes against the grain of the status quo. Peace educators need hardiness and persistence to hold their own. Fortunately, the gains made in peace education over the past decade are a tribute to those very qualities.

Ian Harris, Executive Director of the Peace Education Commission, puts the argument in support of peace education this way: In such a violent world, young people need help in relating their own lives to the violence they see around them. Often they are so distraught by violence that they cannot focus on their lessons. There already exists a solid body of research showing that college students who take conflict resolution classes tend to address issues of daily conflict in their own lives, giving themselves a greater sense of control. Also, conflict resolution education supports the development of resilience in young people. It improves students' social and emotional competency, conflict behaviour, and academic performance. It contributes to a healthy school climate by reducing vandalism, violence, absenteeism, and failure. Young people who receive this form of peace education are less aggressive and more pro-social.

Can learning how to be tolerant, patient, compassionate, kind, and generous be evaluated? How can we prove that young people who have been taught to be flexible, calm, and reflective become proficient at opening up channels of communication and employing alternatives to violence? It is hard to quantify results, just as it is hard to show conclusively that a UN negotiation in a certain country averted a war. We know a fight when we see one, but we are unable to characterize peace. We can recognize a child who is starving or maimed. But it is not easy to credit the precise instrument that has kept a society peaceful or is responsible for apple-cheeked youngsters.

The essence of the culture of peace is mutual respect, understanding, and co-operation. These may seem amorphous, but they are the very qualities that lift up a society from the brutishness of conflict. Love cannot be measured with a yardstick or a scale, yet its absence is always palpable. We can see a fire burning down a building, but are seldom conscious of the prevention methods that avoided one.

Some denigrate what is called "soft power" in international relations, as if the only thing that matters in dealing with the world community is the amount of weaponry a country possesses and the willingness to use it. Soft power relies on influence to achieve a just solution to a problem. It is an intangible and, of course, is frequently bowled over by the heavy tactics of the strong. But the powerful—so often using violence to achieve an end—do not invalidate the qualities of human concern for one another. Peace education is definitely not flabby. Those who believe in it must keep arguing that the criterion for its success is not the same criterion as is used for hard science.

As Boutros Boutros-Ghali, former Secretary-General of the UN, showed in his *An Agenda for Peace*, sometimes force may have to be used to repel an aggressor, but not before every avenue of preventive diplomacy has been used. Peace education promotes the use of preventive diplomacy and, thus, living peacefully on the planet. It gives young people insights into the sources of violence and empowers them to avoid and transform it. "Developing a peace consciousness is a sophisticated task equally as important and difficult as becoming proficient mathematically," Ian Harris says, "but schools tend to neglect this important learning." In the rush to acquire sophisticated academic skills, schools sometimes ignore sophisticated human relations skills that make civilized life possible. The challenge for peace educators is to convince their professional colleagues of the value of teaching about peace.

Practical Education Programs

The Hague Appeal for Peace continues to give vivid testimony of this value. In 1999, upwards of 8,000 people of 100 nationalities gathered in The Hague for a four-day "jamboree" of seminars, exhibits, concerts, and a general outpouring of human yearning for peace. The meeting expressed the view that the coming generation "deserves" a radically different education, one that does not glorify war but educates for peace, non-violence, and international co-operation. It launched the Global Campaign for Peace Education, which produced a three-volume manual, *Learning to Abolish War: Teaching Toward a Culture of Peace,* prepared by the Teachers College, Columbia University Peace Education Team, directed by Dr. Betty Reardon and Professor Alicia Cabezudo, two internationally known educators. The manual, designed for elementary and secondary classroom use, was distributed to 50 countries and translated into several languages. It opens up for teachers ways to approach environmental, ethical, gender, and values issues that are at the heart of peace education.

The main social purposes of peace education we advocate here are the elimination of social injustice, the renunciation of violence, and the abolition of war. War and all forms of violence are interrelated, as evidenced by the culture of violence that surrounds us. War is the core institution of the present global security system, the fount from which pour forth the rationalizations for and habits of violence found in so many aspects of life.

The manual makes a strong case for the development of skills of non-violence to counter the widespread belief that violence is inevitable. It illuminates a wide range of strategies available to educators to teach, in an appropriate manner, the fundamentals of disarmament, non-violent conflict resolution, peacemaking, and peacekeeping. These themes have too long been considered too technical for the average person. No longer. Dr. Reardon says that societies can be transformed if citizens see the possibilities for transformation, if they understand the mechanisms of institutional changes upon which the transformation can be built: "Enabling learners to see these possibilities and to understand these mechanisms is a primary responsibility of the field of peace education for the twenty-first century."

Turning education into action, the Hague Appeal linked with the UN Department for Disarmament Affairs on an "Education for Action" pilot program to demilitarize the mentality of young people and mobilize community support for weapons collection in four countries: Albania, Cambodia, Niger, and Peru. The program trained teachers and community leaders in peace and conflict resolution and related themes, such as communication and problem-solving skills, conflict prevention, tolerance, and the rights and responsibilities of children.

In four other wartorn countries—Kosovo, Somalia, Sudan, and Tajikistan—UNICEF has run post-conflict projects to teach young people about the impact of small arms. Teaching materials on non-violent conflict resolution were developed for school curricula. Education activities then expanded from a focus on the child to the general community in an effort to get a still frightened population to turn in guns.

In other places, civil society leaders have undertaken mine-awareness education to protect the public, and especially children, from the terrors of anti-personnel land mines. In dealing with post-conflict dangers, the UN has found that education programs are vital in disarming former combatants, destroying illicit arms, and training democratic security forces. Special education efforts help women and children, particularly child soldiers, and others severely affected by armed conflict.

Despite problems of funding and professional acceptance, peace education is growing. It struggles to overcome the antiquated charge, left over from the Cold War, that peace education is a left-wing agenda. Peace certainly does not belong to any one political party but ought to be the driving concern of all parties. Sadly, this is not so. Foreign policy is still too widely practised as but the extension of domestic policies. The struggle to deepen political understanding that the world cannot continue to tolerate national states' insistence on their own rights at the expense of others is a long one.

Concerned about the threat of modern wars, ethnic conflict, and environmental destruction, increasing numbers of people are turning to peace education to provide them with knowledge about alternatives to violence. The past decade has seen the production of many books on peace education and hundreds of curricula that contain lessons about raising children with peaceful attitudes and behaviour. Much of the growth in the academic field of peace education can be attributed to scholars associated with the International Peace Research Association, which has established a Peace Education Commission. This body helps educators focus on broad interpretations of peace education—personal peace, interpersonal peace, national reconciliation, environmental sustainability, and conflict resolution. New books are appearing with an international focus on disarmament and human rights, ethnic hatred, domestic crime, interpersonal conflict, and environmental destruction.

The UN study showed ways to lift disarmament and the other elements of global security out of purely academic domains by emphasizing education as a lifelong and multi-faceted process in which the family, schools, universities, the media, communities, NGOs, governments, parliaments, and international organizations all participate. It is a building block—a base of theoretical and practical knowledge—that allows individuals to choose values that reject violence, resolve conflicts peacefully, and sustain a culture of peace.

Numerous groups should be included in this education, including children and youth, school and university students, and educators and trainers; researchers, scientists, engineers, and physicians; and private and corporate donors. It should also include religious and indigenous peoples, and community and municipal representatives; policy makers, such as parliamentarians and government officials; trade unions and the business community; and professionals implementing laws and policies, such as the military and law enforcement agents.

As primary educators of their families and communities, women need to participate in decision-making on disarmament, demobilization, and reintegration programs as well as other peace education and training efforts. The media and NGOs working on peace, disarmament, human rights, environmental, and development issues also play an important role in influencing public opinion.

Resource and enrichment materials need to be adapted and integrated into existing educational or training materials at various levels of education and designed for different audiences. Education programs for children and youth should integrate elements of the culture of peace. In addition to enrichment materials for teachers and students, resource material could also provide primary and secondary education curriculum planners with practical examples of ways to integrate peace education into a range of curricula or teacher training programs.

New curricula should:

- Assist in developing critical skills and critical thinking on the subject

- Take into account that disarmament and non-proliferation education is an integral and essential part of peace education

- Cover all levels of the education system and be adapted to the needs of the various social and economic groups concerned

- Take into account the special cultural, economic, and social characteristics of each country

- Adopt a multidisciplinary approach

- Highlight the human dimensions of conflict, including individual experiences from victims and survivors of war

- Provide a forum for dialogue on conflict reduction, which is essential for achieving the goals of peace education.

The Power of the Internet

A new instrument that has powerfully boosted peace education is the Internet. Exaggerating its importance would be hard, because it is so powerful in bringing information on the vast number of subjects covered by the culture of peace right into our homes. The Internet is the antidote to the mainline media's fixation on the culture of war. The range of information on events, documents, and trends— available instantly—is breathtaking. If knowledge is power, as Sir Francis Bacon said, the average person—seemingly so far removed from the halls of power—has never been so powerful. Of course, people too poor to access the computer world can hardly use the Internet. Still, the oft-heard goal of "a computer in every classroom" could be achieved if governments put more money into the culture of peace than the culture of war.

The Internet may indeed contain junk and some obscenity, but the number of informative Web sites is overwhelming and the number of linkages seemingly infinite. Links to databases are extraordinary resources for research. The wealth of this information grows daily. Just to acquire and digest the information about the actions of hundreds of dynamic civil society groups—information that the mainline media often ignores, bypasses, or downplays—is both encouraging and hopeful and empowers us to participate. The Internet, and its counterpart, the e-mail system, provide access to new audiences in wide-sweeping education programs.

A spectacular example of peace education by means of the Internet is seen in the UN's Cyber School Bus, a global teaching and learning project for students ages five to eighteen and their teachers. Its visual and design techniques provide vast amounts of information in digestible sizes on subjects such as AIDS, biodiversity, child labour, child soldiers, children's rights, climate change, disarmament, drug abuse, governance, human rights, international law, preventing conflict, peacekeeping, poverty, refugees, and technology.

Multimedia tools—including streaming videos, webcasts, chat rooms, and bulletin boards—permit the learner to observe, participate, and network in ways that were unimaginable only a few years ago. Also, high and low technology teaching tools and techniques for conveying content, stimulating interest, and evoking emotions—such as videos, animation, electronic games, theatre, dance, and films—as well as the graphic arts, such as photography, are effective means for presenting the concepts of tolerance, democracy, and conflict resolution. Participatory learning techniques include role-playing or simulation exercises that foster the mind-expanding process of seeing the world through the eyes of others.

The University for Peace

The University for Peace (UPeace) in Costa Rica demonstrates what constitutes peace education now and what it can become in the future. In 1948, Costa Rica was the first country to abolish its army. In that tradition, efforts to establish UPeace began at the UN under the leadership of the President of Costa Rica, Rodrigo Carazo. In 1980, the UN General Assembly approved the charter of the university, and it was set up in some small buildings on a vast hill overlooking tropical-forested valleys in the central plains near the capital city of San José. Its first Chancellor was Robert Muller, former Assistant Secretary-General of the UN and a strong proponent of communicating the value of peace. The university concentrated at first on Latin America and offered a limited number of postgraduate programs on natural resources and human rights.

But almost from the first, it was plunged into financial crisis. Though it was a UN institution, only a few small governments contributed funding and the Western governments virtually refused to have anything to do with it.

In the 1990s, the university languished and only the action of Kofi Annan, when he became Secretary-General, prevented it from closing its doors. In 1999, Annan appointed as Chancellor Maurice Strong, the Canadian entrepreneur who had a long history of holding important UN posts (he was Secretary-General of the 1992 Rio Summit). His challenge was to revitalize the institution. He launched a worldwide campaign for funding from governments and corporations and, in a short period of time, had amassed sufficient funds to enable the university to operate on a $4.5 million annual budget. The Canadian International Development Agency (CIDA) and the UN Foundation became major donors. Though modest by modern university standards, the UPeace budget has given the university intellectual autonomy and was responsible for an influx of professors and students. Strong was able to attract, as the new Rector, R. Martin Lees, a scholar and former UN official who had worked in international co-operation programs in China and Russia. A newly appointed Council of seventeen distinguished figures in education began to fully exercise the Mission of UPeace: "promoting among all human beings a spirit of understanding, tolerance and peaceful co-existence..."

The university now specializes in post-graduate studies in Natural Resources and Conflict Management, International Law and Peace, Human Security, and Disarmament and Non-Proliferation. It has launched a Master's Degree Program in Peace Education with two inter-related goals: capacity building (leadership training) and reform of educational systems (toward peacebuilding education). This will allow students from 50 countries to develop an understanding of the main challenges to peace in the twenty-first century, methodological options available in peace research and conflict resolution, and critical thinking and practical skills for preventive diplomacy, peacekeeping, peacemaking, and peacebuilding. Several departments at UPeace—Natural Resources and Peace, International Law and Human Rights, Gender and Peace, and Human Security—are expanding their credit courses.

A special feature of the university is the partnerships it is developing with a range of universities and institutions across the world to enable UPeace to benefit from the strengths of well-established institutions. Of equal importance is the education material that UPeace provides to educational institutions in developing countries. Strong envisions a "peace research network" to strengthen the linkages among organizations engaged in similar programs in research and education for peace. As part of the UN family, UPeace offers its students career opportunities in a wide range of UN agencies and departments as well as in their own governments.

UPeace is an exciting scholarly development and shows that education can indeed become a new and powerful "weapon" in the long struggle for peace. Peace education will produce new leaders and enlightened citizens who can advance informed and responsible human security initiatives and can generate information that NGOs can use to rouse public opinion. In short, education provides the tools to achieve the goals of good governance, the culture of peace, and full participation in civil society, which is the subject of the next chapter.

9

Civil Society:
New Demands
for a Humane World

A new force has entered world affairs and its name is civil society. Governments are afraid of it. The media does not understand it. The name itself seems vague, and describing what it means is hard to do. Yet it has the potential to drive political processes everywhere toward implementing the elements of a culture of peace. Throughout history, most great social movements, from the abolition of slavery to women's equality, have begun not with governments but with ordinary people. The rise of global civil society in the twenty-first century is preparing the way for a new kind of governance across the world.

The gains that have so far been made in achieving limited disarmament agreements, aid to the developing countries, environmental protection, and advancement of human rights would not have occurred without the push exerted by civil society. Any examination of social progress over the past number of decades will show that leading members of civil society provided the impetus to push governments forward. For example, mothers in Scandinavia, worried about the effects of Strontium 90 from atmospheric nuclear testing on their breast milk, were instrumental in forcing Presidents Kennedy and Khrushchev to negotiate the Partial Test Ban Treaty in 1963. Action by parliamentarians later was instrumental in converting the Partial Test Ban Treaty to the Comprehensive Test Ban Treaty in 1996. Similarly, the thousands of women who showed up at the 1995 Beijing UN Conference on Women were successful in pushing governments to adopt measures to protect the rights of women. The Earth Summit of 1992 in Rio would not have produced the environmental measures it did without the tremendous push of non-governmental organizations (NGOs) that were present in the thousands. The leadership of civil society groups is also widely credited with the achievements of the Anti-Personnel Landmines Treaty and the International Criminal Court.

Civil society activism in advancing social justice has reached a new level of involvement and is now empowering millions of persons around the world in bringing forward their concerns. This was obvious in the highly visible global dialogue preceding the 2003 Iraq war, in which civil society questioned the very legitimacy of the war itself for close to one year before it was actually waged. Around the world, literally millions of people of all ages, political opinions, and cultures took to the streets in peace marches and demonstrations in the days before the attacks began. Never before had this happened on such a grand scale before a war actually started. Robert Muller, former Assistant Secretary-General of the UN and Chancellor Emeritus of the University for Peace, sees this as a stunning new era of global listening, speaking, and responsibility. He said:

> No matter what happens, history will record that this is a new era, and that the 21st century has been initiated with the world in a global dialogue looking deeply, profoundly and responsibly as a global community at the legitimacy of the actions of a nation that is desperate to go to war.

Although this new determinism is dramatically challenging the political order, the expressions of concern appear to the media to be diffuse, and thus they do not receive sustained or thoughtful media attention. Politicians still treat such representations as mere "special interest groups." Others are either preoccupied with their own concerns or have dismissed the advancement of the human security agenda as something beyond their control. Yet growing numbers of people, dissatisfied with the failure of governments to resolve conflicts and produce equitable development standards, are beginning to look at the world in ways that they never did before. This is the beginning of systemic change.

The Growth of NGOs

The term "civil society" is sometimes confused with NGOs, a more familiar designation of people who, for the most part, volunteer their service to an organization with a cause. Some NGOs, like the United Nations Association, spread information; some, like Project Ploughshares, critique government policies; and others, like CARE and Save the Children, provide humanitarian relief. Some NGOs work in their own community while others are part of international networks. NGOs have been around for a long time. Representatives of 1,200 voluntary organizations were present at the founding conference of the UN in 1945. They played a significant role in writing the first seven words of the Charter: "*We the peoples of the United Nations ...*" and also Article 71, providing that "the Economic and Social Council (ECOSOC) may make suitable arrangements for consultation with nongovernmental organizations."

Since the UN began, the number of international NGOs has grown enormously, with more than 37,000 at work today. They embrace virtually every level of organization: from the village community to global summits, and from the provision of micro-credit and the delivery of emergency relief supplies to environmental and human rights activism. Within the UN system, more than 2,000 NGOs have consultative status with ECOSOC, and 1,400 with the Department of Public Information. More than 3,500 NGOs were given formal accreditation at the 2002 Johannesburg Summit on Sustainable Development.

In recent years, three trends have converged to change this rather formal designation of NGOs. First, the string of UN conferences on all major global problems—from food and housing to energy and disarmament—unleashed a torrent of civic involvement that spilled far beyond traditional NGOs. Second, the growing awareness that national governments alone were not solving human security problems occurred at the same time democracy itself was spreading across the world. Consequently, people began to desire to have more and more self-determination about the future of world development. And third, the explosive growth and advance in Internet technology has enabled individuals and civil society groups to co-ordinate their agendas and actions across long distances and without censorship. In his book *Smart Mobs*, Howard Rheingold says the new communication technology greatly enhances the power of social networks to the point where new forms of co-operative social action, never before possible, are becoming the order of the day.

The result of these trends has been an explosion of civic involvement: protests, seminars, books, partnerships, electronic communication, and consciousness-raising events. The age of civil society has been born. The list of actors is very long and includes: academic institutions, business forums, consumer advocates, development co-operation initiatives, environmental movements, ethnic lobbies, faith-based associations, human rights activists, labour unions, local community groups, peace movements, philanthropic foundations, professional bodies, relief organizations, think tanks, women's networks, and youth associations.

NGOs certainly stand out in this panoply, but the new civil society stretches much further than the formally organized, officially registered, and professionally administered NGOs. It is impossible to measure this universe of activity. It certainly numbers in the millions, from tiny village cooperatives to global activist organizations, such as Greenpeace. One indication of the size of this force was seen in the ten million people in many countries who marched on February 15, 2003, against war in Iraq. The diversity of the new activists was seen in the elderly couple in the London march carrying a placard that said "Make tea, not war!"

The range of these groups' work, as Jessica T. Mathews, Senior Fellow at the US-based Council on Foreign Relations, points out in an article entitled "Power Shift," is almost as broad as are their interests. "They breed new ideas; advocate, protest, and mobilize public support; do legal, scientific, technical, and policy analysis; provide services; shape, implement, monitor, and enforce national and international commitments; and change institutions and norms."

Two broad characterizations of civil society might be said to be those who work within the structural processes of the UN, and those who work outside the traditional systems. They are not mutually exclusive by any means. The fluidity of civil society is one of its hallmarks.

Working Within the System

The first track of civil society participates in governmental arenas in an effort to influence governmental decisions. They crowd the basement corridors of the UN headquarters in New York where they lobby delegates, hold seminars and workshops, and track various UN committee meetings. Sometimes, accredited delegates with special competence address the meetings. When the UN holds international conferences on various themes, NGOs spearhead parallel meetings where experts suggest ideas on what should be done. Many governments include civil society representatives in their delegations to international conferences and frequently also to the General Assembly. UN treaty bodies now routinely consider alternate reports from NGOs alongside the official reports of governments. Sometimes, NGOs even give testimony to Security Council members about specific crises, though usually outside official meetings.

These gains for NGO participation in the daily affairs of the UN have not been easy. And as their numbers and competency increase, resistance to their entry grows. Some states in Africa, Asia, and Latin America find NGO prodding and exposure of human rights violations annoying. Some powerful European, North American, and East Asian states resent NGO pressure for economic justice, disarmament, and global democracy. In the disarmament field, the major states severely limit the access of NGOs that, in many instances, know considerably more about the details of disarmament discussions than the delegates.

NGOs are continuing to push for access to meetings dealing with ways to strengthen the UN system, its financial situation, and Security Council reform, but governments jealously guard these fields for themselves. Governments are all too aware that there are deep disagreements between states and specific NGOs on particular issues. On the odd occasion when an NGO outburst of protest has taken place, governments have used incidents of acrimonious behaviour as a reason for exclusion (a tactic that has increased since September 11, 2001). Governments are also arguing, and Kofi Annan has had to take note, that the explosive growth in NGOs is crowding the facilities. It is now physically impossible to accommodate all NGOs requesting participation in UN meetings. Much of the pressure for admittance is coming from the industrialized countries, but the developing countries are also experiencing a surge in the number of NGOs, and the latter are especially feeling the pressures of exclusion.

Fortunately, the UN's Web site provides up-to-the-minute information on the hundreds of topics the UN deals with simultaneously, so there is no need to be present at the UN to receive information. But an NGO has to be on the premises and in the meetings, if only as an observer, to have input into the deliberations, to benefit from exchanges with other NGOs, and to bridge the chasm between the civil society perspective and that of government delegates (whose professional lifestyle immerses them in a sort of cocoon). To get along with the institutional process, NGOs must constrain their criticism and put up with the tedious tenets of diplomacy in which progress is often measured in the minutest details of draft texts.

This patience does have its rewards. Just before the 2000 UN Millennium year, Kofi Annan, clearly a friend of and believer in NGOs, convened a five-day NGO Forum to provide input into the governmental summit to take place a few months later. Annan called the gathering "the NGO Revolution" because it went far beyond protesting against the dark side of globalization; civil society can become the "new superpower" in building worldwide campaigns to strengthen multilateral norms and develop legal regimes.

To calm government fears that NGOs would soon be marching through the UN, Annan's office felt it necessary to issue a statement that the Secretary-General's support of the NGO Forum was a one-time event. But already there is pressure for some sort of second assembly open to representatives of "the people." Most who propose a second assembly see it as something that will evolve from an ad hoc annual event into a permanent organization, perhaps even established through a charter amendment. The financial limitations of the UN, the deluge of crises and world problems that sap the time and energy of the organization (not to mention the Secretary-General and his staff), and the government resistance to any encroachment on their authority make it unlikely that we will see a second assembly soon. If it does happen, it is more likely to be composed of parliamentarians who have a higher claim to be representative.

The big question that NGOs and the rest of civil society still have to answer is: Whom do they represent? True, they represent groups with special interests and competencies, but to whom in the electorate of a democracy are they accountable? Will the day ever come when a "People's Assembly" of the UN is directly elected by peoples around the world? What is certain is that civil society is a catalytic force that is not always welcomed by governments, especially when civil society challenges the system itself.

Working Against the System

The second track of civil society is less disciplined, less constrained, often volatile in its criticism, and frequently deeply creative. Nowhere is this collection of civil society more visible than at the World Social Forum.

In 1998, the draft of a Multilateral Agreement on Investments (MAI) was made public. The draft, discussed in secret negotiations among Western governments, would have given the world's wealthiest countries even more power over the economies of developing countries. The French newspaper *Le Monde Diplomatique* exposed the negotiations, an outcry from the public followed, the French government withdrew, and the negotiations collapsed.

At this same time, protest movements against the overbearing decisions of the international financial institutions—notably the International Monetary Fund (IMF), the World Bank, and the World Trade Organization (WTO)—began to gather more supporters. The rallying cry was "globalization," at least the dark side of it, in which self-interested capitalism imposes its rule and hegemony over the most vulnerable nations and peoples.

In 1999, key individuals in the campaign to defeat the MAI gathered to create a shadow event to the World Economic Forum (WEF), an elite meeting of world economic and political leaders held each year in Davos, Switzerland. This annual gathering of corporate titans and their political friends has become famous. Since 1971, the WEF has played both a symbolic and a real leadership role in shaping the global economy. It is based in a Swiss foundation funded by more than 1,000 multinational corporations. To counter this economic dominance, activists in the global justice movement began to challenge the notion that there is no alternative to corporate-led globalization. More than protest, they sought the development of concrete alternatives.

The World Social Forum (WSF) was born in January 2001, and to date three world gatherings of activists have been held in the southeastern Brazil port city of Porto Alegre. The first gathering drew 20,000 participants; the second, about 50,000; and the third, in 2003, well over 100,000 from 126 countries. Participants included social activists, political organizations, women's groups, peace activists, human rights campaigners, development NGOs, and trade unions. They brought a shared understanding of the roots of poverty, inequality, hunger, environmental degradation, wars, and human rights violations. The WSF has become an open meeting place where groups and movements of civil society opposed to neo-liberalism and a world dominated by big business engage in debate, formulate proposals, share their experiences, and network for effective action. The theme of the gatherings has been "Another World Is Possible."

The style of the WSF is somewhat eclectic. It operates in a decentralized fashion without any locus of power. The social movements represented at Porto Alegre maintain their own programs, drawing their unity in the common conviction that the work of promoting human rights, social justice, and democracy has many starting points. Forum participants say their experience in such a joyful, robust setting offers the hope that overcoming violence, wars, subjugation, hate, and fear in the world is more than an idealistic dream.

The featured speakers at the 2003 meeting, Noam Chomsky and Arundhati Roy, were given rock star treatment, with thousands turning out to hear them. Chomsky, the Massachusetts Institute of Technology (MIT) professor who is internationally known for his withering criticism of US foreign policy, rejected the idea that the "masters of the universe" (a reference to the rich countries that make up the WEF) could control the world agenda. Roy, the Indian novelist and social critic, said: "Another world is not only possible, she is on her way. On a quiet day, I can hear her breathing." The new President of Brazil, Lula da Silva, told the cheering crowd, "I will tell the people at Davos that the world does not need war, the world needs peace and understanding." He then flew to the Davos meeting and did exactly that.

The WSF represents civil society at its most robust, and the 2003 meeting saw a merging of the global justice and peace movements. These non-state actors and social activists transcend national boundaries and consider themselves global citizens foremost. They consider the nation state to be outmoded or insufficiently responsive to the transcending problems of globalization. Though the nation state still has immense power—it runs wars—its decision-making processes are increasingly being challenged by the emerging global civil society.

The contours of civil society are hard to map. Civil society relies on "soft power," rather than hard, and it ebbs and flows. But at the very least, it is an alternative to the globalization preferred by the big business interests represented at Davos. That alternative presents a new kind of power.

No longer can governments operate in elitist ways, making their decisions as if the masses were too unsophisticated to understand the nuances of policies. Civil society leaders are highly informed and made even more so by a daily stream of information, electronically conveyed, that was never before available. This ascendancy of civil society comes just at the time when the forces of globalization—which I prefer to call the interdependence of nations and peoples around the world—are reducing the former absolute power of the nation state.

Today, the major problems of human security—development, disarmament, environment, and human rights—are interlocked. No one problem can be solved alone. And no single state can solve problems by itself. An integrated agenda for human security demands co-operation by all nations. Civil society has had the best understanding of the essential unity of the world that is manifest in the present crises. The fate of humanity itself is at the centre of these crises. And it is civil society, not governments, that is leading the way to a more humane world.

We must remember, of course, that every social movement has its dark side. Civil society includes destructive elements such as racists and religious fundamentalists who seek to deny the democratic rights of others. It also has within it a small element of anarchists whose idea of a good day is to confront the police with violent action. Since the police in some places are all too ready to employ their truncheons and tear gas to disperse protesters, the provocation is sometimes mutual. When confrontation occurs, the TV cameras are there in a flash and the images sent out around the world are of bloodied protesters smashing police barricades and tearing down fences, as occurred when the Asia Pacific Economic Cooperation met in Quebec City in 2001. The public sees the violence and then—without any other knowledge as the basis of their opinions—associates protest marches with criminal behaviour. This is what occurred at protests in Seattle, Genoa, and Quebec City. What went almost unnoticed in Genoa, where a protester was killed by the police, was that serious issues were being debated: a tax on investment transactions, the alleviation of Third World debt, the rights of migrants and refugees, and the opening of the European market to agricultural produce from outside. Civil society workshops on these subjects were virtually ignored by the media.

While anarchists exploit peaceful protests for their own purposes, the overwhelming number of those who turn out to protest the deprivations inflicted by the international financial institutions on so many in the world want to do so in a peaceful manner. Better co-operation between civil society leaders and the police reduces the potential for violence. But the downside is that media coverage of the positive side of civil society's activism also declines; 24-hour news stations thrive on images of conflict. Porto Alegre, for all its severe criticism of the policies of capitalism, has been devoid of violence, as have the meetings where civil society works within the system.

Two Tracks: One Message

The two tracks of civil society—those working inside the government systems and those working against—are each sending out essentially the same messages. They address the need for a just and lasting peace in the world, the eradication of poverty, a course of sustainable development for humanity while protecting a shared environment, and the upholding of human rights. These are, of course, the values of the culture of peace, and they hold the promise of making globalization benefit all.

Which route is more likely to achieve the goal? The UN Millennium Forum represents an evolutionary approach; Porto Alegre a radical one. The first is tame, respectful, and somewhat elitist; the second is brash, irreverent, and loud.

The first wants to inspire and co-operate with governments; the second distrusts and confronts them. The UN route waits to be recognized by officials; Porto Alegre waits for no one. Porto Alegre at the UN is hard to imagine.

A choice between the two is not necessary. The UN route has the potential for improving, in a more human way, the work of the structures. Porto Alegre wants the very structures—at least those of the international financial institutions—changed. The clamour and pressure from without increases the opportunity of those within to be heard. Both the UN and Porto Alegre routes are needed.

Without a doubt, radical change in international politics is essential to reverse the present trend lines of the war culture. The poor of the world and those being killed in the endless parade of wars need someone to speak up on their behalf. The modern crises demand a profound reform of all the international institutions and strengthening of the UN system. "We the peoples of the United Nations" deserve a multilateral system based on universal ethical principles. It is doubtful that this can be realized only from within government systems. Yet there must be links to the systems, and that is what the UN route provides.

Many NGOs pursue both approaches. The Hague Appeal for Peace produced a huge rally at The Hague, challenging governments to change their approach to human security issues, and then set to work within the UN system in a number of partnership programs with governments. The Lawyers Committee for Nuclear Policy and associated bodies produced a Model Nuclear Weapons Convention and then worked with governments to get it formally introduced into the UN. Anti-personnel land mines advocates struck up a working relationship with the Government of Canada ("the Ottawa Process") to complete a Landmines Treaty. World Federalist Movement leaders worked closely with many governments to bring about the International Criminal Court. The Middle Powers Initiative, composed of representatives of international organizations highly critical of governments' nuclear weapons policies, sends delegations to present briefs and engage in dialogue with governments at high levels.

The summation of all this work—from within and from without—puts pressure on government systems to change. Clearly, a social revolution is occurring in which, from a hundred avenues, civil society leaders are manifesting humanity's deep desire for inclusion. Whether this new phenomenon can become a new superpower in the world, as is sometimes contended, remains to be seen. What is certain is that a new critical assessment of governments is seeping through the populace.

Already, civil society is effectively challenging the hierarchy of old power with the new power of worldwide networks. The marginalization of women, which has long kept half the world's people from decision-making meetings, has given way to a new surge of women's active involvement in peace issues. Women were the driving force behind UN Security Council Resolution 1325, passed on October 31, 2000, which calls for the greater participation of women in all decision-making levels of governments.

The mistrust of governments today is palpable. Rising civil society movements are challenging the political elitism that has caused so much discord and suffering. This free-wheeling, centreless spurt of social activism, fed by instant worldwide electronic communication, provides hope for change. Governments may seem at times impervious to change, but it is unlikely that even the most recalcitrant ones could resist much longer if civil society ever became unified and relentless in its demands for a more humane world.

Conclusion

When "We the Peoples" Demand Peace

Notre Dame Cathedral in Paris, soaring with a perfection all its own, is a magnificent religious edifice and one of the supreme masterpieces of French art. Construction of the present church, built on the ruins of its predecessors, began in 1163 during the reign of Louis VII. Generations of stonemasons, carpenters, ironsmiths, sculptors, and glaziers gradually built the foundation, the walls, the flying buttresses, vaulting, roofing, and finally the towers of the huge church. The building was not completed until 1345.

The history of Westminster Abbey in London goes back to the sixth century. The present church was begun in 1220, when Henry III started construction of the Lady Chapel. The transept, choir, the first bay of the nave, and the chapter house were not completed until late in that century. Work then came to a halt and another two centuries passed before the nave was finished.

The Holy Mosque in Makkah, the most revered place for Muslims around the world, has been expanded several times throughout history to accommodate the growing number of pilgrims for the annual hajj. Successive Islamic regimes spared no expense or effort to dignify and honour the Mosque. The two million pilgrims who flock to the modern setting, which was completed only in 1992, benefit from the labours of those who worked on the structure over a thousand-year period.

Through many parts of the world, the grandest architectural achievements of the great cathedrals, mosques, and temples testify to the ingenuity, skill, and toil of generations of dedicated people. It took decades, sometimes a century or more, for the grandeur of each to unfold. The craftsmen who laid the stones in the foundation did not live to see the whole structure and wonder at the power of their creation. Yet if they had not done their work meticulously, day by day, to ensure that every stone was precisely secured, the rising edifice would never have withstood the passing storms. That they would never see the end result of their work did not matter. They had seen the design, they knew a step-by-step process was required, and they believed that every small detail of their work had value.

So, too, building a culture of peace requires daily dedication to fulfill the vision. We must have the patience of those who laboured on the great edifices, content just to participate without expecting to see the end product. Patience is not, however, a quality associated with the modern world. We live in an age of "instant everything": instant coffee, fast food, electronic communication, supersonic flight, and space travel. We insert raw steel into an assembly line and out comes an automobile. But human beings are not instant anything. And neither are we robots.

The incessant violence of the ages has programmed us to think of wars as the inevitable outcome of conflict. We are defensive and suspicious of others. The adaptation of human beings—to change images of the enemy into understanding and tolerance, to replace armaments with disarmament, to stop exploiting the weak and the environment, and to practise sustainable development—takes a long time.

The time required to educate and transform sufficient numbers of individuals so that they embrace the culture of peace conflicts with the necessity of getting the job done now. The trend lines of population growth, resource scarcities, the rising demands of the oppressed, and the proliferation of weapons of mass destruction mean that we are dealing with a finite window of opportunity to resolve world issues. How then do we reconcile the fact that human beings cannot be reprogrammed instantly with the new urgencies of the culture of peace? This question can lead to an agonizing of the human spirit, and then perhaps to a lapse into lethargy. The great virtues of faith, hope, and love have never been needed so much as they are needed now to cope with the challenge confronting us.

Certainly, the complexities of our time defy a simple answer, let alone the formulation of one policy for all. Still, the list of 50 Ways to Build World Peace shows how an individual can approach large issues by small and meaningful actions. "Teaching your children about peace" and "aiding the starving" are not only achievable today, but can have a profound effect on the future. The list of 50 Ways may appear to suggest simple actions, but they are certainly not simplistic.

---

50 Ways to Build World Peace

Take your share of responsibility for the world
Send letters to newspapers
Welcome strangers
Be friends with your neighbours
Write to world leaders
Avoid blaming others
Mediate a conflict
Smile at people when you're walking
Start a petition
Seek mutual understanding
Take action!
Aid the starving
Live simply so all can simply live

Instead of fighting, forgive
Create a world for grandchildren
Teach your children about peace
Learn new ways
Stand up against bullying
Join peace protests
Help those in need
Educate others
Exercise tolerance
Meditate
Cultivate inner peace
Talk about peace
Know that your actions matter!
Wear a peace badge
Help provide what's missing
Protest at arms sales
Campaign against war
Write to local politicians
Share what you have
Care for your environment
Organize a peace rally
Support hunger charities
Have a loving attitude
Do voluntary service overseas
Become an activist
Speak up for peace
Think positively
Participate
Aim so everyone wins
Be open minded
Listen before you react to anger
Consider others
Actively support peace initiatives
Exchange ideas
Help others be heard
Believe that you can make a difference
Speak out against prejudice

Laurie Phillips
International Community Action, UK
Used with permission

To have continuing effect, the unleashing of human energy called for by this list must be anchored in three fundamental ways that can move society from a culture of war to a culture of peace. We must *understand, participate, and communicate*.

Understand

When we fully understand the meaning of the photo of the Earth sent back by astronauts—in which we see this beautiful, fragile sphere as a whole—an attitudinal change occurs. Though we continue to live on the streets of our own community, the image of the entire planet lifts up our thinking. Who are the people on the other side of the globe? What are they doing? What is their daily life like? This awakening to the concerns of others leads us into the sources of vast amounts of information now available about food, water, health, jobs, and other human problems faced by those in different societies. This information, available from a vast network of UN sources, leads us further into the zones of intolerance, discrimination, conflicts, and wars. Questions follow. Why is there so much starvation when there is so much food in the world? Why do we tolerate the existence of nuclear weapons, which threaten to destroy the processes of life? Why are we polluting the atmosphere and waters when we have the technology to avoid this? Why do we have the UN and then refuse to empower it to stop wars and end starvation?

The first sign of real knowledge is to examine the quality of the questions it evokes. In previous centuries, we were not able to frame questions large enough to address fully the nature of the human condition. While there have always been visionaries, many of whom made the scientific and technological breakthroughs that allowed the astronauts to take the photo of the Earth, the public as a whole did not share in visionary thinking. The ordinary person has always been caught up in the mundane tasks of daily existence. What concerns our family and our business this week, not the state of the global community 25 years from now, has monopolized our attention. But now the flow of information, electronically conveyed, opens up new vistas for everyone. Many still live within the confines of their own "world," but many more now extend their thinking about the world to places far beyond their neighbourhood. The questions posed by this larger view, held by growing numbers of the public, are a sign of the change in attitudes that is occurring. This new attitude is the first requisite of a culture of peace.

Participate

I referred in Chapter 9 to the emergence of the new civil society. This is truly one of the great phenomena of our time. If people who belonged to NGOs once felt on the margins of the decision-making processes, civil society now effectively injects itself into public policy debates. The rate of participation is a direct corollary of the flow of information. "Smart mobs" are the twenty-first century vehicle for people power. The combination of a world attitude developed by flows of information and the number of people involved in the new forms of social interaction is a power the world (and certainly the politicians) has not seen before.

Many politicians are worried about the state of democracy because of declining voter turnout at elections. They are missing the point. Many, particularly the young, are bypassing the traditional political processes precisely because they are so antiquated and incapable of solving contemporary security problems. The more direct actions of civic involvement—to express one's opinion and link with like-minded individuals across the globe—are more appealing. Today, democracy does not equal political involvement. That is a huge change in thinking that I myself have witnessed during 30 years in public life. Democracy is thriving as never before.

The "hierarchy" of political direction is coming to an end, if it is not already finished. The trouble President George W. Bush had in getting his war against Iraq started illustrates that leaders, no matter how powerful, can no longer just commit entire societies to war. The power of people, who now understand the measures available to resolve conflicts in a fair and just manner without violence, has asserted itself. That it did not win the day on the Iraq issue does not deny the increasing influence of civil society in shaping the future. Again, this bodes well for the development of a culture of peace.

Communicate

Understanding and participation inevitably lead to communication. Communicating is what we constantly do now. Marshall McLuhan may have been right a generation ago when he said: "The medium is the message." But he would have to update his aphorism today. The message now uses the medium. I do not refer to the mainline media, which, like the political structure, is still locked in a corporate mentality that regards the public as nothing more than avaricious, mentally deficient consumers. The mainline media thrive on confrontation, whether in fiction or real life, and cunningly feed the baser instincts we all have. Mainline media outlets are not as important anymore to those who have discovered the powers of alternate communication, from the cell phone to text messaging. The Internet is the centrepiece of the revolution in electronic communication. It is the base of new ways of receiving information, from UN documents to chat rooms where social activists converge.

The Internet is not the message. The message is that we no longer need the mainline media to inform us about what is going on in the world. Civil society has a message and employs the new medium to transmit knowledge on a mass scale—knowledge that is unfiltered by editors who have the interests of their own medium largely in mind as they make daily decisions about what we will see or read. People highly knowledgeable in the elements of the culture of peace have a hard time getting access to the mainline media, but the specialists in the culture of war are seen all the time. The mainline media still treat war as an adventure. Alternative media delve into the creativity required for peace. In the new medium, peace is explained widely; war is criticized.

This does not mean that advocates of the culture of peace should ignore the mainline media. Quite the reverse. They should send letters to the editor, contribute articles for the op-ed pages, phone radio call-in shows, and express their views in the polls increasingly done by media. They should, in short, seek to balance the war coverage with peace coverage. They need to speak up so that editors learn that there are significant sections of the audience who want to hear about the important themes of peace. Often the knowledge gained from alternative sources is the factor that enables and emboldens individuals to speak out publicly.

Not Seeing the Blossom

This book is premised on the belief—which the UN has stated—that the peoples of the world have a sacred right to peace. We must insist on this truth and let no one dissuade us from it by the false claims of "impracticality." Nothing is more practical. Gandhi showed the power of non-violent resistance to social injustice. The time has come to resist the greatest social injustice—the institution of war. For war will kill us all. The only way humanity can survive is by overcoming the culture of war, which has brought us to the unacceptable state of now being the authors of our own destruction.

If, in previous times, it could be said that humanity did not possess the tools of peace but only the tools of war, that condition no longer exists. The UN gives us the base of international law to resolve human conflict. No government or group can any longer legitimately employ the old concept of a "just war" in pursuit of its goals.

We have not yet reached sufficient maturity of civilization to enforce the right to peace. Governments, at least some of them, are still too strong and are able to overcome the wishes of those who have turned against war. But this situation will not prevail forever. It will give way to those who demand the right to peace, just as the forces of slavery, colonialism, and apartheid gave way when the opposition became strong enough. That is why developing the elements of a culture of peace—education, sustainable development, respect for all human rights, equality between men and women, democratic participation, understanding and tolerance, free flow of information, and human security for all—is so important. A culture of peace will not only make the world a more human place, it will lead inexorably to the acquisition of the human right to peace. Future generations, when they have tasted the fruit of a culture of peace, will recognize almost intuitively that peace is their right. They will demand it. Our role, as the twenty-first century begins, is to nourish the seeds of peace so that the blossom appears.

The full blossom may not appear until my grandchildren, or their grandchildren, have grown up. I accept the prospect that I will not see the blossom. The immediate goal is for every generation to ensure that there will be a following generation. The advance of civilization thus far tells me that humanity is not fated for oblivion; indeed, the new interconnected human community is a source of strength to continue building the culture of peace. I must feel this strength so that I can talk and write, in realistic terms, of achieving the human right to peace. I do feel the strength. The strength of this moment gives me hope for the future, and hope is itself a powerful motivation for action. This hope for a decent future for humanity must awaken a universal sense of responsibility. When "we the peoples" seize this responsibility, the human right to peace will be assured.

Appendix

The Human Right to Peace

Declaration by Federico Mayor
Former Director-General of UNESCO
January 1997

Lasting peace is a prerequisite for the exercise of all human rights and duties. It is not the peace of silence, of men and women who by choice or constraint remain silent. It is the peace of freedom—and therefore of just laws—of happiness, equality, and solidarity, in which all citizens count, live together, and share.

Peace, development and democracy form an interactive triangle. They are mutually reinforcing. Without democracy, there is no sustainable development: disparities become unsustainable and lead to imposition and domination.

In 1995, the fiftieth anniversary of the United Nations and UNESCO and the United Nations Year for Tolerance, we stressed that it was only through a daily effort to know others better—I am the 'other'!—and respect them that we would be able to tackle at source the problems of marginalization, indifference, resentment, and hatred. This is the only way to break the vicious circle that leads from insults to confrontation and the use of force.

We must identify the roots of global problems and strive, with imagination and determination, to check conflicts in their early stages. Better still prevent them. Prevention is the victory that gives the measure of our distinctively human faculties. We must know in order to foresee. Foresee in order to prevent. We must act in a timely, decisive, and courageous manner, knowing that prevention engages the attention only when it fails. Peace, health and normality do not make the news. We shall have to try to give greater prominence to these intangibles, these unheralded triumphs.

A universal renunciation of violence requires the commitment of the whole of society. These are not matters of government but matters of State; not only matters for the authorities, but for society in its entirety (including civilian, military, and religious bodies). The mobilization which is urgently needed to effect the transition within two or three years from a culture of war to a culture of peace demands co-operation from everyone. In order to change, the world needs everyone. A new approach to security is required at world, regional and national levels. The armed forces must be the guarantors of democratic stability and the protection of the citizen, because we cannot move from systems of complete security and no freedom to systems of complete freedom and no security. Ministries of war and defence must gradually be turned into ministries of peace.

Decision-making procedures and measures to deal with emergencies must be specially designed to ensure speed, co-ordination and effectiveness. We are prepared for improbable wars involving the large-scale deployment of inordinately costly equipment, but we are not equipped to detect and mitigate the natural or man-provoked disasters that occur repeatedly. We are vulnerable to the inclemency of the weather, to the vicissitudes of nature. The protection of the citizen must be seen as one of the major tasks of society as a whole if we really wish to consolidate a framework for genuinely democratic living. Investing in emergency help and relief measures and— above all—in prevention and the long term (for example, in continent-wide water distribution and storage networks) is to be prepared for peace, to be prepared to live in peace. Currently, we are prepared for possible war, but find ourselves surprised and defenceless in our daily lives in the face of mishaps of all kinds.

The United Nations system must likewise equip itself with the necessary response capacity to prevent the recurrence of atrocities and instances of genocide such as those which today afflict our collective conscience— Cambodia, Bosnia and Herzegovina, Liberia, Somalia and Rwanda...

There is today a general desire for peace, and we must applaud the clear thinking and strength of mind displayed by all the warring parties in the accords that have been reached in El Salvador, Namibia, Mozambique, Angola, South Africa, Guatemala and the Philippines. These agreements fill us with hope but also sadness, when we think of the lives sacrificed on the long road to the cease-fire, and of the open wounds, so difficult to heal. Thus, as we revive the concept of the 'construction of peace in the minds of men', we now call on all adversaries who still put their trust in weapons to lay down their arms and seek reconciliation.

Condemnation will not suffice. It is time for action. It is not enough to feel outrage when we learn of the number of children exploited sexually or at work, of refugees or of those suffering from hunger. We must react, *each of us* to the best of our abilities. It is not just a matter of looking at what the government is doing. We must part with something of 'our own'. We must give, give of ourselves. We must stop imposing models of development, models for living. The right to peace, to live in peace, implies jettisoning the belief that some are virtuous and correct while others are wrong, and that some are always giving while others are always in need.

It is clear that we cannot simultaneously pay the price of war and the price of peace. Guaranteeing lifelong education for all would enable us to: control population growth, improve the quality of life, increase civic participation, reduce migratory flows, level out differences in income, assert cultural identity and prevent the destruction of the environment through substantial changes in energy use patterns and urban transport; promote endogenous development and the transfer of knowledge; foster the swift and effective operation of justice, with appropriate machinery for international co-operation; provide the United Nations system with appropriate facilities to tackle transnational problems in time. None of this can be achieved in a context of war. What is needed, then, is to reduce the investment in arms and destruction in order to increase investment in the construction of peace.

The distillation of traditions, thoughts, languages, forms of expression, memories, things forgotten, wishes, dreams, experiments, rejections, culture finds its supreme expression in our everyday behaviour. Infinite cultural diversity is our great resource, which is underpinned— this is our strength—by universal cultural values that must be passed on from the cradle to the grave. Family members—especially mothers—teachers, the media, everyone must help to spread the ethical principles, the universal guidelines that are so necessary today for haves and have-nots alike: the latter because they have a right to the basic minimum standards that human dignity demands; the more fortunate because material goods fail to deliver the expected pleasure. Where there is no longing, possession brings no enjoyment. In education, tools are useful. But nothing can replace the friendly words of a teacher, or the caresses and smiles of parents. The only real education is education by example … and love.

Learning without frontiers—whether geographical, or frontiers of age or language—can help to change the world, by eliminating or reducing the many barriers that today impede universal access to knowledge and education. Education must help to strengthen, reclaim and develop the culture and identity of peoples.

Globalization carries with it a danger of uniformity and increases the temptation to turn inwards and take refuge in all kinds of convictions—religious, ideological, cultural, or nationalistic. Confronted with this threat, we must 'emphasize the forms of learning and critical thinking that enable individuals to understand changing environments, create new knowledge and shape their own destinies'. Indigenous peoples must be placed on an equal footing with other cultures, participating fully in the drafting and application of laws. Peace means diversity, a blending—of 'hybrid, wandering cultures' as Carlos Fuentes put it; it means multi-ethnic and multilingual societies. Peace is not an abstract idea but one rooted firmly in cultural, political, social, and economic contexts.

Above all, this profound transformation from oppression and confinement to openness and generosity, this change based on the daily use by all of us of the verb 'to share—which is the key to a new future—cannot be achieved without our young people, and certainly not behind their backs. We must tell them—they who represent our hope, who are calling for our help and who seek in us and in external authorities the answers to their uncertainties and preoccupations—that it is in themselves that they must discover the answers, that the motivations and glimpses of light that they are seeking can be found within themselves. Although at times it may be difficult, given both their consternation and our own, to present the situation to them in those terms, our position as lifelong teachers and learners obliges us to say to young people, as Cavafy put it in a poem: 'Ithaca gave you the journey. . . She has nothing left to give you now'. Each according to his own plan. Each according to his own way of thinking. Free from self-serving outside interference, especially when it robs the young of their own 'core', the intellect, talent, and resourcefulness which are the most precious individual and collective treasure of humankind. Sects and the escape provided by drug addiction are the clearest symptoms of this pathological state of mind that is our great problem today. Indeed, education means activating this immense potential and using it to its fullest so that each may become the master and architect of his or her own destiny. We cannot give to youth what we no longer possess in youthful vitality, but instead we can offer what we have learned through experience, the fruit of our failures and successes, of the burdens, joys, pain, and perplexity and the renewed inspiration of each new moment.

Let youth hold high the banner of peace and justice! So convinced am I of the relevance of this goal to the proper fulfilment of our mission that I have proposed to the General Conference that it designate 'UNESCO and youth' as a central topic for discussion at its next session. That will be an appropriate moment since the General Conference will be considering for adoption the 'Declaration on the Safeguarding of Future Generations'.

At all the United Nations conferences, regardless of the subject under consideration (environment, population, social development, human rights and democracy, women, housing), there has been a consensus that education is the key to the urgently needed change in the direction pursued by today's world, which is increasing disparities in the possession of material goods and knowledge, instead of reducing them. To invest in education is not only to respect a fundamental right but also to build peace and progress for the world's peoples. *Education for all, by all, throughout life: this is the great challenge.* One which allows of no delay. Each child is the most important heritage to be preserved. UNESCO may at times give the impression that it is only interested in preserving stone monuments or natural landscapes. That is not true. Those efforts are the most visible. And the heritage thus safeguarded the least vulnerable. But we must protect our entire heritage: the spiritual, the intangible, the genetic heritage – and, especially, ethics.

These are the basic, universal values that our Constitution sets forth with inspired clarity. If we sincerely believe that each child is our child, then we must radically change the parameters of the 'globalization' currently under way. And the human being must become the beneficiary and main actor of all our policies and strategies.

A system collapsed in 1989 because, concentrating on equality, it forgot liberty. The present system, focused on liberty, will know the same fate if it forgets equality—and solidarity. The din made as the 'Iron Curtain' collapsed drowned out the tremor that ran through the foundations of the 'winning' side in the Cold War. We must, then, for the sake of both principle and self-interest, redouble in every field the fight against exclusion and marginalization. We must all feel involved. We must all work to ease the great transition from the logic of force to the force of reason; from oppression to dialogue; from isolation to interaction and peaceful coexistence. But first we must live, and give meaning to life. *Eliminating violence: that is our resolve.* Preventing violence and compulsion by going, as I said before, to the very sources of resentment, extremism, dogmatism, and fatalism. Poverty, ignorance, discrimination, and exclusion are forms of violence which can cause—although they can never justify—aggression, the use of force and fratricidal conflict.

A peace consciousness—in the interests of living together, of science and its applications—does not appear overnight, nor can it be imposed by decree. First comes disillusionment with materialism and enslavement to the market, and then a return to freedom of thought and action, sincerity, austerity, the indomitable force of the mind, the key to peace and to war, as affirmed by the founders of UNESCO.

Science is always positive, but the same cannot always be said of its applications. Advances in technology and knowledge can be used to enrich or to impoverish the lives of human beings; they can help to develop their identity and enhance their capacities or, on the contrary, they can be used to undermine the personality and coarsen human talent. Only conscience, which is responsibility—and thus ethical and moral—can make good use of the artefacts of reason. Conscience must work in tandem with reason. To the ethics of responsibility we must add an ethics of conviction and will. The former springs from knowledge, and the latter from passion, compassion and wisdom.

We are now approaching the end of a century of amazing scientific and technological progress: we can diagnose and treat many diseases which cause suffering and death; we communicate with extraordinary clarity and speed; we have at our disposal instant, limitless information. However, antibiotics and telecommunications do not compensate for the bloody conflicts which have cut down millions of lives in their prime and inflicted indescribable suffering on so many innocent people. All the obscenities of war, brought home to us nowadays by audio-visual equipment, do not seem able to halt the advance of the huge war machine set up and maintained over many centuries. Present generations have the almost impossible, biblical task of 'beating their swords into ploughshares' and making the transition from an instinct for war— developed since time immemorial—to a feeling for peace. To achieve this would be the best and most noble act that the 'global village' could accomplish, and the best legacy to our descendants. With what satisfaction and relief should we be able to look into the eyes of our children! It would be also the best way to celebrate the fiftieth anniversary of the Universal Declaration of Human Rights, in 1998.

Other 'rights' have been added since 1948. These should all be taken into account, and to them should be added the right which underlies them all: the right to peace— the right to live in peace! The right to our own 'personal sovereignty', to respect for life and dignity.

Human rights! At the dawn of the new millennium, our ideal must be to put them into practice, to add to them, to live and breathe them, to relive them, to revive them with every new day! No one nation, institution, or person should feel entitled to lay sole claim to human rights, still less to determine others' credentials in this regard. Human rights can neither be owned nor given, but must be won and deserved afresh with every passing day. Nor should they be regarded as an abstraction, but rather as practical guidelines for action which should be part of the lives of all men and women and enshrined in the laws of every country. Let us translate the Declaration into all languages; let it be studied in every classroom and every home, all over the world! Today's ideal may thus become the happy reality of tomorrow! Learning to know, to do, to be, and to live together!

In these first days of the new year—a time for taking stock and making plans—I appeal to all families, educators, religious figures, parliamentarians, politicians, artists, intellectuals, scientists, craftworkers, and journalists, to all humanitarian, sporting and cultural organizations, and to, the media to spread abroad a message of tolerance, non-violence, peace and justice. Our aim must be to foster understanding, generosity, and solidarity, so that with our minds more focused on the future than on the past, we may be able to look ahead together and build, however difficult the conditions or inhospitable the setting, a future of peace, which is a fundamental right and prerequisite. Thus, 'We, the people' will have fulfilled the promise we made in 1945, our eyes still seared by the most abominable images of the terrible conflict that had just ended—'to save succeeding generations from the scourge of war', 'to construct the defences of peace in the minds' of all the peoples of the Earth.

Chapter Notes

Chapter 1

Summaries of the wars of the twentieth century are found in Project Ploughshares Armed Conflict Reports 1997–2002 www.ploughshares.ca/content/ACR/acr.html, the World Political Almanac (Checkmark Books), and the BBC "Wars and Conflict" Series www.bbc.co.uk/history/war. The report of the Carnegie Commission on Preventing Deadly Conflict is located at http://wwics.si.edu/subsites/ccpdc/pubs/rept97/finfr.htm. A poignant description of war today is found in *The Impact of War on Children* by Graca Machel (London: Hurst, 2001). Good resources on Afghanistan include *Veiled Threat: The Women of Afghanistan* by Sally Armstrong (Toronto: Penguin, 2002), the 2001 and 2002 Amnesty International reports on Afghanistan, Afghanistan Online www.afghan-web.com, and the Institute for Afghan Studies at www.institute-for-afghan-studies.org/Body.htm.

For the section on Iraq, I found articles in *The London Free Press* (February 8, 2003) and *The Montreal Gazette* (January 4, 2003) very informative. Fareed Zakaria provides an insightful analysis of the international community's opposition to US policies in the March 24, 2003, edition of *Newsweek* magazine. A good overview of the Just War Theory is contained in the Internet Encyclopedia of Philosophy www.utm.edu/research/iep/j/justwar.htm. The *Constitution on the Church in the Modern World*, one of the sixteen principal documents of the Second Vatican Council, provides the essential Catholic teaching on war. The extent of violence in the world today is revealed in the "World Report on Violence and Health" published by the World Health Organization Geneva (2002). "The Seville Statement on Violence" was published by UNESCO www.unesco.org/cpp/uk/

declarations/seville.pdf. The International Commission on Intervention and State Sovereignty was established by the Government of Canada in September 2000 and chaired by Gareth Evans and Mohamed Sahnoun. The Commission's report is available at www.dfait-maeci.gc.ca/iciss-ciise.

Chapter 2

In 1987, the World Commission on Environment and Development, chaired by former Prime Minister of Norway Gro Harlem Brundtland, issued a global call to action for strategies to promote development without further degradation of the environment. This key idea is captured in the term "sustainable development," which, the Commission explained, "seeks to meet the needs and aspirations of the present without compromising the ability to meet those of the future."

A description of the Earth Summit in Rio in 1992 is contained in my earlier book, *A Bargain for Humanity* (Edmonton: University of Alberta Press, 1993). Figures for the opportunity costs of militarism are in *GAIA: An Atlas of Planet Management* (Toronto: Doubleday, 1993). Data on military spending is provided by the Stockholm International Peace Research Institute, http://projects.sipri.se/milex.html. The 2003 UN Human Development Report can be found at www.undp.org/hdr2003.

The statement "Battle for the Planet," issued by Nobel Peace Laureates on the eve of the Johannesburg Summit, is found at www.greencrossitalia.it/ita/speciali/johan/battle.htm. The 2002 UN document *Global Challenge, Global Opportunity: Trends in Sustainable Development* provides a good overview of world conditions; it can be found at http://image.guardian.co.uk/sys-files/Guardian/documents/2002/08/13/Unreport.pdf. Readers are directed to the Final Document of the 1987 UN Conference on the Relationship Between Disarmament and Development, which is at disarmament.un.org/cab/docs/aconf13039.pdf. The document *Military Effect on the Environment,* published by the International Peace Bureau, is particularly insightful. At Johannesburg, the Global People's Forum issued a statement listing the steps toward sustainable development that governments should take. The analysis of the Johannesburg Summit by Lucy Webster,

Executive Director of Economists Allied for Arms Reduction, in the organization's October 2002 Newsletter is helpful. The UN Human Development Report 1994 has an excellent chapter, "Capturing the Peace Dividend." The UN Food and Agriculture's report on hunger is located at www.fao.org/DOCREP/005/Y7352e/Y7352e00.htm. "The World Health Report 2002," published by the World Health Organization, is useful. Valuable information on the water crisis is contained in "Global Water Outlook to 2005: Averting an Impending Crisis," published by the International Food Policy Research Institute, Washington, D.C. (September 2002) and also *Resource Wars: The New Landscape of Global Conflict* by Michael T. Klare (New York: Metropolitan Books, Henry Holt & Co., 2001). Climate change information is contained in *State of the World 2002* (New York: W.W. Norton & Co., 2002). HIV/AIDS information is in the UNAIDS 2002 document, "Report on the Global HIV/AIDS Epidemic," and "The Future of AIDS" by Nicholas Eberstadt, *Foreign Affairs*, Nov.-Dec. 2002).

Chapter 3

The text of the Non-Proliferation Treaty (NPT), the most important arms control and disarmament treaty in the world, can be found at www.un.org/Depts/dda/WMD/treaty. My earlier book, *An Unacceptable Risk* (Waterloo, ON: Project Ploughshares, 1995), deals with the NPT indefinite extension, and a later book, *The Ultimate Evil* (Toronto: Lorimer, 1998), comments on the 1996 Advisory Opinion of the International Court of Justice concerning the legal questions of nuclear weapons. The quote from Bruce Blair is from *The Defense Monitor* published by the Center for Defense Information (May 2002). The warning by Jayantha Dhanapala, former Under-Secretary-General for Disarmament Affairs, is in his speech given upon receiving the Alan Cranston Peace Award from the Global Security Institute, April 16, 2002. The text of President Bush's new "National Security Strategy" is located at www.whitehouse.gov/nsc/nss.html.

The Nuclear Posture Review (NPR) was announced at a Pentagon press briefing on January 9, 2002. The report was not made public, but portions have been leaked to the press, and substantial excerpts can be found at www.globalsecurity.org/ wmd/library/policy/dod/npr.htm. I have drawn on the analysis of the NPR by Jeffrey Boutwell, Executive Director of Pugwash, in his paper "The U.S. and No First Use: Preemption Trumps Deterrence?" (October 30, 2002), found at www.pugwash.org/ reports/nw/outwell.htm. The New Agenda Coalition resolution—which was adopted November 22, 2002, with 118 in favour, 7 opposed, and 38 abstaining—is found at A/C.1/57/ L.2/Rev. 1: www.reachingcriticalwill.org/1com/1com02/res/ L2rev1.html. For an analysis of the NATO review of its nuclear weapons policies, see www.ploughshares.ca/CONTENT/ WORKING%20PAPERS/wp013.html The Final Document of the UN First Special Session on Disarmament in 1978 is at http:/ /disarmament.un.org/gaspecialsession/10thsesmain.htm.

A detailed description of how terrorists could acquire and use nuclear weapons is contained in "Nuclear Nightmares" by Bill Keller, *The New York Times Magazine*, May 26, 2002. The same author followed up this article with another, "The Thinkable," *The New York Times Magazine,* May 4, 2003, which describes the new age of "usable" nuclear weapons. And, an unusual source, *National Geographic,* has published a compelling "Special Report: Weapons of Mass Destruction" by Lewis M. Simons, which provides an ominous description of future attacks (November 2002). *Popular Mechanics*, which also does not usually deal with these issues, published "Tiny Nukes: America's New Weapons of Precise Destruction Are the Cornerstone of Our First-Strike Strategy" (October 2002). Dr. Sean Howard, editor of *Disarmament Diplomacy*, provides insights into nanotechnology in "Nanotechnology and Mass Destruction: The Need for an Inner Space Treaty" (Issue 65, July/August 2002). Background material on the threat of biological and chemical warfare is contained in material published by the Department of Foreign Affairs and International Trade, Ottawa.

Chapter 4

Material on Mahatma Gandhi has been taken from "The Imperial Period," "Gandhi and the Struggle for Independence" in *Culture and*

Geography, Beyond Books, and found at www.beyondbooks.com/ wcu91/6j.asp, and on Martin Luther King, Jr. from his biography at www.stanford.edu/group/King/about_king/biography, and the collection of his sermons at www.stanford.edu/group/King/ publications/sermonsFrame.htm. I am indebted to David Adams, who made available to me his personal account, "Annotated Bibliography of Documents Concerning Culture of Peace Along with an Introduction and Conclusion." I have drawn from his notes with his permission. Adams' article, "Moving from a Culture of War to a Culture of Peace," published by the Fellowship of Reconciliation, www.forusa.org, is an excellent summary. As I noted in the chapter, *Crossing the Divide: Dialogue Among Civilizations* (South Orange, N.J.: Seton Hall University School of Diplomacy and International Relations, 2001) is an important contribution to understanding that the diversity of humanity is a gift, not a threat. The material on Federico Mayor was taken from his book *The New Page,* by Federico Mayor and Tom Forstenza (Paris: UNESCO Publishing). The Declaration and Programme of Action on a Culture of Peace is contained in UN Document A/53/243, October 6, 1999. The Executive Board of UNESCO has provided a useful summary of the implementation of the activities of the International Year for the Culture of Peace in its document 161 EX/17, Paris, April 19, 2001. A comprehensive outline of the many facets of the Culture of Peace is provided by UNESCO at www3.unesco.org/iycp/uk/uk_sum_cp.htm. Two further UN documents were particularly helpful: the Report of the Secretary-General on the International Decade for a Culture of Peace and Non-Violence for the Children of the World, A/ 55/377, September 12, 2000, and the text of the resolution on this theme, A/55/47, November 29, 2000.

Chapter 5

The UN Declaration on the Right of Peoples to Peace is contained in UN Document A/Res/39/11, November 12, 1984, and is found at www.un.org/documents/ga/res/39/a39r011.htm. The Report by the Secretary-General on the Human Right to Peace is available at http://unesdoc.unesco.org/images/0011/ 001100/110027e.pdf. I consider Federico Mayor's statement on the Human Right to Peace to be such a succinct and moving argument that I am reprinting it as an Appendix to this book. The Report by the Director-General on the Human Right to Peace given to UNESCO's General Conference is a helpful summary of the debate on the issue and also contains the draft of the Oslo Declaration on the Human Right to Peace (UNESCO Document 29/C/59, October 29, 1997). The UN Declaration on the Right to Development was adopted December 4, 1986: www.un.org/documents/ga/res/41/a41r128.htm. The Vienna Declaration and Programme of Action, issued by the World Conference on Human Rights, was published by the UN Department of Public Information, New York, DPI/1394-39399, August 1993. In explaining the Convention on the Rights of the Child, I have drawn on UNICEF material: www.unicef.org/crc/crc.htm. The document prepared by Lawyers for Social Responsibility, "Legality of the Use by a State of Nuclear Weapons in Armed Conflict," is an excellent summary of legal questions concerning the human rights aspects of nuclear weapons. It is available at www.peacelawyers.ca/Documents/IntLawNWProfs.htm. The Farewell Speech by Mary Robinson, former UN High Commissioner for Human Rights, gives a helpful assessment of the state of human rights today: http://193.194.138.190/huricane/huricane.nsf/view01/608B646C44611148C1256C31002FF3E8?opendocument.

Chapter 6

As a multi-pronged institution, the UN cannot be fully grasped in any one book or document. I have drawn chiefly on my own experience in working and attending conferences at the UN for 30 years. However, the UN's Web site, www.un.org, is an excellent entry point into an appreciation of the scope of the organization. I have not tried to tell the story of the UN here; I did that in an earlier work, *United Nations: Divided World* (NC Press, 1984). Rather, I have expressed my viewpoint on how the UN is a natural vehicle to carry humanity forward into an era of a culture of peace. That the UN has weaknesses is indisputable. Its performance in Bosnia and Rwanda was dismal. David Rief has exposed some of these weaknesses in his book *A Bed for the Night:*

Humanitarianism in Crisis (New York: Simon & Schuster, 2002). My view is that by far the biggest problem of the UN is the lack of support it receives from its member governments.

UN Secretary-General Kofi Annan's document *We the Peoples: The Role of the United Nations in the Twenty-first Century*, is available at www.un.rg/millennium/sg/report. A companion document is "Declaration and Agenda for Action: Strengthening the United Nations for the Twenty-first Century," the final document of the People's Millennium Forum, www.un.org/millennium/declaration.htm. An interesting profile of the Secretary-General and the Organization is contained in "The Optimist," by Philip Gourevitch, *The New Yorker*, March 3, 2003, p.50. Kofi Annan's acceptance speech on receiving the Nobel Peace Prize shows the value of the UN to humanity, especially after September 11, 2001. It is available at www.nobel.se/peace/laureates/2001/annan-lecture.html. "The ABCs of Disarmament: The UN's Disarmament Machinery," by William Epstein, was published by the non-governmental organization (NGO) Committee on Disarmament: http://disarm.igc.org. The text of the McCloy-Zorin Accords can be found at the Nuclear Age Peace Foundation Web site: www.nuclearfiles.org/redocuments/1961/610920-mccloy-zorin.html.

Chapter 7

An excellent overview on the role of religion in the modern world is contained in *Toward a Global Civilization? The Contribution of Religions*, edited by Patricia M. Mische and Melissa Merkling (New York: Peter Lang Publishing, 2001). The book was the outcome of a symposium conducted by Global Education Associates, New York, in 1997. The chapters on Islam by three different authors—Saleha Mahmood-Abedin, Abdul Aziz Said, and Nathan C. Funk—are particularly valuable in understanding the true nature of Islam. The book *Taking Back Islam: American Muslims Reclaim Their Faith*, edited by Michael Wolfe (Emmaus, PA: Rodale, 2002), effectively answers those who reacted to the terrorism of September 11, 2001, by blaming Islam. Karen Armstrong, perhaps the leading non-Muslim scholar on Islam, has valuable chapters in the book. I have also drawn from Ms.

Armstrong's book *The Battle for God* (New York: Ballantine Books, 2000) in my discussion of religious fundamentalism. The inaugural issue of *Voices Across Boundaries*, May 2003, www.acrossboundaries.net/voices, is devoted to the subject "Killing for Our Beliefs." It explores the complex question of why some kill in the name of God or Truth. As the interview with Seyyed Hossein Nasr, a distinguished authority on Islamic spirituality, shows, violence against others is not inherent in Islam's teachings.

The World Conference on Religion and Peace has a helpful Web site, www.wcrp.org, which takes the viewer through more than three decades of work done to foster a stronger religious presence in peace issues. Although the second World Parliament met 100 years later, the intervening years saw the launch of a number of interfaith organizations: the International Association for Religious Freedom, the World Congress of Faiths, the Temple of Understanding, the World Interfaith Association, the World Conference on Religion and Peace, the National and International Council of Churches, the International Council of Christians and Jews, and the Pontifical Council for Inter-Religious Dialogue. Each of these groups has made its own contribution to advancing understanding and joint activity among people of faith. Their stories are reviewed in Marcus Braybrooke's book *Pilgrimage of Hope: One Hundred Years of Interfaith Dialogue* (New York: Crossroad, 1992). The Parliament of the World's Religions has a Web site, www.cpwr.org, and the text of the 1993 "Declaration of the Religions for a Global Ethic" is also contained in *Toward a Global Civilization? The Contribution of Religions*. Hans Küng provides background information on the document at http://astro.temple.edu/~dialogue/Center/kung.htm. I have also drawn from Küng's thinking as expressed in his book *Global Responsibility: In Search of a New World Ethic* (New York: Crossroad, 1991). The report of the Commission on Global Governance is published as a book, *Our Global Neighbourhood* (New York: Oxford University Press, 1995). It is a far-seeing document that I have used for several years as a text in my seminars at the University of Alberta. Though I do not agree with all the philosophy of Yale Professor Peter Singer, I found his book *One World: The Ethics of Globalization* (New Haven, CT: Yale University Press, 2002) useful. And of course, my frequent references to *Crossing the Divide: Dialogue among Civilizations* (South Orange, NJ: Seton Hall University, 2001) indicate my high regard for its contents. Material on the "Ethical Globalization Initiative," a new venture to support human rights begun by Mary Robinson, is found at www.eginitiative.org. The participants in the UN's Dialogue Among Civilizations, in addition to Küng, were: Dr. A. Kamal Aboulmagd, Egypt; Dr. Lourdes Arizpe, Mexico; Dr. Hanan Ashrawi, Palestine; Dr. Ruth Cardoso, Brazil; The Honourable Jacques Delors, France; Dr. Leslie Gelb, US; Nadine Gordimer, South Africa; His Royal Highness Prince El Hassan bin Talal, Jordan; Professor Sergey Kapitza, Russia; Professor Hayao Kawai, Japan; Professor Tommy Koh, Singapore; Graca Machel, Mozambique; Professor Amartya Sen, India; Dr. Song Jian, China; Dick Spring, T.D., Ireland; Professor Tu Weiming, China; The Honourable Richard von Weizsacker, Germany; Dr. Javad Zarif, Iran; and Giandomenico Picco, Italy, Personal Representative of Secretary-General Kofi Annan, for the United Nations Year of Dialogue Among Civilizations.

Chapter 8

Professor Ian Harris and John Synott were the guest editors for the January 2002 special issue of *Social Alternatives*, a quarterly multi-disciplinary journal that analyzes contemporary social, cultural, economic, and ecological developments and is committed to equality, democracy, and social justice. Eleven articles of the issue took up the theme "Peace Education for a New Century" and provide an excellent overview of the subject. The article "Globalization and University Peace Education" by Anne Adelson (*Peace Review* 12:1, 2000) is also helpful. I have drawn from my address "Peace, Humanity, Equality: The Challenge for Peace Education," to the Annual Conference for Peace Education in Canada at McMaster University, Hamilton, Canada, November 9, 2002, which was also used in the chapter "Learning to Build Peace" in *Sustainable Peace* (Edmonton: University of Alberta Press, 2003). "Learning to Abolish War: Teaching Toward a Culture of Peace," A Peace Education Resource Packet Based on the Hague Appeal for Peace and Justice for the Twenty-first Century, was developed by Betty A. Reardon and Alicia Cabezudo (Hague Appeal for Peace, 777 UN Plaza, New York 10017). *Educating for a Peaceful Future* (Toronto: Kagan and Woo, 1998), edited by David C. Smith and Terrance R. Carson, provides an excellent overview of peace education, including its history and a chapter of practical activities. Meetings of the Peace Education Commission have produced a variety of anthologies that have played a key role in advancing peace education as a legitimate realm within educational disciplines. They include *Handbook on Peace Education* (Frankfurt: International Peace Research Association, 1974), *Three Decades of Peace Education Around the World* (New York: Garland, 1996), a special edition of the *Peabody Journal of Education* entitled "Peace Education in a Postmodern World" (1996), and a special issue on Peace Education in *New Horizons*, the journal of the World Education Fellowship (2000). The UN Study on Disarmament and Non-Proliferation Education, tabled in the UN on October 9, 2002, provides very helpful information for educators and a list of recommendations for both government and NGO action. "The Meaning of Global Education," a paper prepared by the Canadian International Development Agency, discusses the attitudes that should be formed in students. An excellent teaching kit, *Learning to Abolish War: Teaching Toward a Culture of Peace*, is available for order at www.haguepeace.org/index.php?name=pagetool_news&news_id=41. The 2003 Prospectus of the University for Peace in Costa Rica, www.upeace.org/prospectus2003.pdf, provides a clear sense of direction of where peace education is headed. The Hague Appeal for Peace education program is found at www.haguepeace.org/index.php?name=education.

The UN's CyberSchoolBus may be found at www.un.org/Pubs/CyberSchoolBus/index.asp. Another important educational initiative is Schoolnet, www.schoolnet.ca, a Canadian government-sponsored Web site for schools.

The University for Peace has also received funding from the Governments of Costa Rica, Denmark, Finland, Germany, Italy, the Netherlands, Norway, Sweden, Switzerland, and the US, as well as from the Dutch Post Code Lottery, the Philanthropic Collaborative, American University, SIDA Sweden, IDRC Canada, DSI Germany, and Inclusion International.

Chapter 9

Howard Rheingold's book *Smart Mobs:The Next Social Revolution* was published in 2003 by Perseus (Cambridge, MA). Jessica T. Mathews' article "Power Shift," in *Foreign Affairs* (Jan./Feb. 1997), explains why governments are unable to ignore the new phenomenon of civil society.A good description of the evolution of NGOs since the UN began is contained in "The Emerging Roles of NGOs in the UN System: From Article 71 to a People's Millennium Assembly," by Chadwick Alger, published in *Global Governance,* vol. 8, no. 1 (2002), pp. 93-117.The same publication published "From 'Consultative Arrangements to Partnerships':The Changing Status of NGOs in Diplomacy at the UN" by Peter Willetts (6.2, 2000), pp. 281-304. "Who's Minding the Store? Global Civil Society and Corporate Responsibility" by Melanie Beth Oliviero and Adele Simmons provides a comprehensive examination of how civil society is affected by the September 11 terrorism; it was published in *Global Civil Society 2002* (New York: Oxford University Press, 2002), pp. 77-107. I found "Civil Society and Democracy in Global Governance" by Jan Aart Scholte in *Global Governance,* vol. 8, no. 3 (2002), pp. 191-212, very helpful.The statement given to the Millennium Summit at the UN by Techeste Ahderom, Co-chair of the Millennium Forum, is found at www.onecountry.org/e121/ MF Speech to Millennium Summit.htm, The history of the Porto Alegre movement is contained in "Porto Alegre and Beyond" (Interhemispheric Resource Center, November 2002). The text of the speech given at the 2003 meeting of the World Social Forum by Noam Chomsky is found at www.zmag.org/ content/showarticle.cfm?SectionID=40&ItemID=2938 and Arundhati Roy is found at www.zmag.org/content/ showarticle.cfm?SectionID=51&ItemID=2919.

The World Forum of Civil Society Networks, "UBUNTU," has a Web site: http://ubuntu.upc.es/pag.php?lg=eng.

Helpful Web Sites

Much of the information in these pages was obtained through instantaneous access to documents, initiatives, and activities of international organizations and civil society involved in public policy debates. The Internet is a powerful tool for social change and is spreading exponentially into every corner of the world. It is increasing the scope of knowledge and extending the reach of information sharing; it provides access to vast databases of analyses, data, and resources. It promotes increased communication and interaction among people from all walks of life and is already being used to build a culture of peace.

The following Web sites proved valuable as I was writing this book.

Arms Control Association
www.armscontrol.org
The Arms Control Association is a non-partisan organization dedicated to promoting public understanding of and support for effective arms control policies. This site provides policy-makers, the press, and the interested public with authoritative information, analysis, and commentary on arms control proposals, negotiations and agreements, and related issues.

Canadian Centres for Teaching Peace
www.peace.ca
The Canadian Centres for Teaching Peace is a non-profit organization that seeks to raise awareness of peace issues and to equip individuals to participate in peacebuilding,

beginning in their local communities. Peace.ca is a Web site that facilitates networking and information-sharing, and provides a forum for the development of partnerships to advance peace.

Center for Civil Society Studies
www.jhu.edu/~ccss
The Center for Civil Society Studies of the Johns Hopkins Institute for Policy Studies encourages the development and effective operation of civil society organizations. The Center carries out its work through a combination of research, training, and information-sharing both in the US and around the world.

Common Dreams
www.commondreams.org
Common Dreams is a US non-profit citizens' organization committed to being on the cutting-edge of using the Internet as a political organizing tool—and creating new models for Internet activism.

Council for a Parliament of the World's Religions
www.cpwr.org
The mission of the Council for a Parliament of the World's Religions is to cultivate harmony between the world's religious and spiritual communities and foster their engagement with the world and its other guiding institutions to achieve a peaceful, just, and sustainable world.

Culture of Peace News Network
http://cpnn-new-england.org
Culture of Peace News Network USA is a site of the Culture of Peace News Network, a global network of interactive Internet sites in many languages for information exchange on events and media productions that promote one or more

of the eight keys of a culture of peace. It is a project of the United Nations International Decade for a Culture of Peace and Non-Violence for the Children of the World.

Fundación Cultura de Paz
www.fund-culturadepaz.org/eng/english.htm
The Fundación Cultura de Paz was founded in March 2000 under the chairmanship of Federico Mayor Zaragoza, former Director-General of UNESCO. It was under his direction that UNESCO created the Culture of Peace Program. The Fundación's objective is to contribute to building and consolidating a culture of peace through reflection, research, education, and on-the-spot action. Its activities focus mainly on linking and mobilizing networks of institutions, organizations, and individuals that have a proven commitment to the values of the culture of peace.

Global Movement for a Culture of Peace
www.culture-of-peace.info
Dr. David Adams is the former Director of UNESCO's Unit for the International Year for the Culture of Peace. His responsibilities have included development of national culture of peace projects, research and development of the culture of peace concept, and training in peacebuilding and conflict resolution. This Web site presents some of the key papers from his research.

Global Security Institute
www.gsinstitute.org/index.shtml
The Global Security Institute (GSI) targets influential stakeholders, networks, and decision-makers to promote incremental steps that enhance security and lead to the global elimination of nuclear weapons.

Hague Appeal for Peace
www.haguepeace.org
The Hague Appeal for Peace is an international network of peace and justice organizations. It is dedicated to sowing the seeds for the abolition of war through implementing the Hague Agenda for Peace and Justice for the Twenty-first Century, a set of 50 recommendations developed at the Hague Appeal for Peace Conference in 1999.

Independent Media Centre
www.indymedia.org
The Independent Media Center is a network of collectively run media outlets to create radical, accurate, and passionate truth telling. It works out of an inspiration for people who continue to work for a better world, despite corporate media's distortions and unwillingness to cover the efforts to free humanity.

International Commission for Intervention and State Sovereignty
www.dfait-maeci.gc.ca/iciss-ciise/menu-en.asp
The independent International Commission on Intervention and State Sovereignty was established by the Government of Canada in September 2000 to respond to the UN Secretary-General's challenge to the international community to find consensus on the principles of humanitarian intervention. The Commission's report, *The Responsibility to Protect*, is part of the response to this challenge.

Middle Powers Initiative
www.middlepowers.org
The Middle Powers Initiative (MPI), a central program of the Global Security Institute, is co-sponsored by eight prominent international organizations specializing in nuclear disarmament. MPI sends delegations to middle power

governments to encourage them to press the nuclear weapons states to fulfill their obligations to the Non-Proliferation Treaty. It also holds strategy consultations with government officials and NGOs.

MoveOn.org
www.moveon.org
MoveOn is a catalyst for a new kind of grassroots involvement, supporting busy but concerned citizens in finding their political voice. Its nationwide network of more than 600,000 online activists is one of the most effective and responsive outlets for democratic participation available today.

Project Ploughshares
www.ploughshares.ca
Project Ploughshares undertakes research, education, and advocacy programs that promote the peaceful resolution of political conflict, demilitarization, and the provision of security based on equality, justice, and sustainable environment. The organization publishes the quarterly *Ploughshares Monitor,* which reports on current issues related to militarism and the arms race, as well as the annual *Armed Conflicts Report,* which describes all major armed conflicts worldwide.

Reaching Critical Will for Nuclear Disarmament
www.reachingcriticalwill.org
Reaching Critical Will for Nuclear Disarmament, an initiative from the Women's International League for Peace and Freedom (WILPF), was created in 1999 with a view to increasing the quality and quantity of NGOs in nuclear non-proliferation and disarmament. The site provides an up-to-date list of current disarmament diplomacy, including key documents.

Season for Nonviolence
www.agnt.org/snv02.htm
A Season for Nonviolence, January 30 – April 4, is a national 64-day educational, media, and grassroots campaign dedicated to demonstrating that non-violence is a powerful way to heal, transform, and empower our lives and our communities. Inspired by the 50th and 30th memorial anniversaries of Mahatma Gandhi and Dr. Martin Luther King, Jr., this international event honours their vision for an empowered, nonviolent world.

United Nations
www.un.org
The 191-member UN is the only multilateral organization whose membership approaches universality and whose agenda encompasses all areas of human activity in every region of the world. It is, in effect, the marketplace at which much of the world's multilateral diplomacy is conducted, the mechanism through which the views of the international community are given expression. It is meant as the forum in which members' grievances are aired and resolved. This Web site is updated throughout the day.

United Nations Centre for Disarmament Affairs
http://disarmament.un.org
The United Nations Centre for Disarmament Affairs provides full information on global disarmament bodies and meetings, such as the First Committee, Disarmament Commission, and the Conference on Disarmament. The major international instruments on disarmament are available.

United Nations' Cyber School Bus
www.un.org/Pubs/CyberSchoolBus/index.asp
Part of the UN site, Cyber School Bus provides user-friendly information on the workings of the UN and provides project materials, facts, resources, quizzes, features, and forthcoming events. Colourfully packed with educational activities, it is an excellent resource for teachers and students.

United Nations Development Program's Human Development Report
http://hdr.undp.org
The Human Development Report was first launched in 1990 with the single goal of putting people back at the centre of the development process in terms of economic debate, policy, and advocacy. The goal was both massive and simple, with far-ranging implications—going beyond income to assess the level of people's long-term well-being. Follow this link to the latest report.

United Nations Educational, Scientific and Cultural Organization (UNESCO)
www.unesco.org
UNESCO was established on November 16, 1945. Its headquarters are in Paris, with field offices and units in different parts of the world. The main objective of UNESCO is to contribute to peace and security in the world by promoting collaboration among nations through education, science, culture, and communication. It aims to further universal respect for justice, for the rule of law, and for the human rights and fundamental freedoms that are affirmed for the peoples of the world—without distinction of race, sex, language, or religion—by the Charter of the UN.

United Nations Educational, Scientific and Cultural Organization's Culture of Peace

www3.unesco.org/iycp

As the lead UN agency for the culture of peace, UNESCO maintains an interactive Web site detailing the initiative, including links to official documents and related projects at the local level.

United Nations University

www.unu.edu

The United Nations University, founded in 1973, uses research and capacity-building to find original, forward-looking solutions to the most pressing problems that concern the UN, its peoples, and member states. The University's Web site has been designed to give Internet users direct access to University research, training, and dissemination activities.

University for Peace

www.upeace.org

The University for Peace (UPeace), located in Costa Rica, is committed to developing academic programs that contribute to the culture of peace. The school has an innovative curriculum that includes programs in Natural Resources and Conflict Management, International Law and Settlement of Disputes, Human Rights, Peace Education (educating the educators), Gender and Peace Building, and Economic Development and Security. New areas under development are Environmental Security, Media and Peace, Human Security, and Disarmament and Non-Proliferation. Both the student body and the faculty of UPeace are international and multicultural.

World Conference on Religion and Peace
www.wcrp.org

The World Conference on Religion and Peace (WCRP) is the largest international coalition of representatives from the world's great religions who are dedicated to achieving peace. Respecting cultural differences while celebrating our common humanity, WCRP is active on every continent and in some of the most troubled places on earth, creating multi-religious partnerships that mobilize the moral and social resources of religious people to address their shared problems.

World Social Forum
www.forumsocialmundial.org.br/home.asp

The World Social Forum is an open meeting place where groups and movements of civil society opposed to neo-liberalism and a world dominated by capital or by any form of imperialism, but engaged in building a planetary society centred on the human person, come together to pursue their thinking, debate ideas democratically, formulate proposals, share their experiences freely, and network for effective action.

Z Communications
http://zmag.org

A major alternative media site, Z Communications is made up of an Internet site, magazine, media institute, and videos offering critical thinking on political, cultural, social, and economic life in the US and around the world.

Index of Proper Names and Organizations